CW01657760

A Sheffield Turner's Tale

Life with an unsung hero of steel

Sue Allott

YouCaxton Publications
Oxford & Shrewsbury

Copyright © Sue Allott 2019

The Author asserts the moral right to
be identified as the author of this work.
ISBN 978-1-913425-08-1

Published by YouCaxton Publications 2019
YCBN: 01

All rights reserved. No part of this publication may be reproduced, stored in a retrieval system, or transmitted in any form or by any means, electronic, mechanical, photocopying, recording or otherwise, without the prior permission of the author.

This book is sold subject to the condition that it shall not, by way of trade or otherwise, be lent, resold, hired out or otherwise circulated without the author's prior consent in any form of binding or cover other than that in which it is published and without a similar condition including this condition being imposed on the subsequent purchaser.

YouCaxton Publications
enquiries@youcaxton.co.uk

Contents

Preface

At the foot of Sheffield's majestic Town Hall steps the proud and famous names are embossed on five-pointed stars. Beneath our feet the city's most famous sons and daughters are honoured as 'Sheffield legends'. There are actors and musicians, scientists and artists, well-known names from the world of sport, pioneers in their many achievements. Many of them are not simply famous in their chosen fields but so often embody in their down-to-earth modesty and kindness the best characteristics of the people of Sheffield. All of them are people to be proud of who richly deserve the recognition they receive, the stars that shine brightly to keep their names in all our minds.

But they are not the ones who built this city.

So who did?

The stark answer is that we don't know. Generations of workers who made the wealth of this city, who produced the goods, who developed the skills that made Sheffield famous, are simply anonymous. Worse still, when the policies of the 1980s led to the collapse of industry, the shock was so sudden and so profound that no-one was thinking about history. The steelworks disappeared at breakneck speed, the massive walls of corrugated iron torn down, the bricks and mortar felled by the wrecking ball. As firms went to the wall the carefully kept records of workers, jobs, skills, were suddenly worthless and, as the factory walls came down, were simply thrown out. We do not know who the people were who made the steel, the records of their working lives were, for the most part, simply tossed into a skip.

People left the steelworks and vanished into the anonymous army of unemployed, or found whatever work they could, or, more often than not, left the city forever. The stories of tens of thousands of working lives were lost, the names disappeared, and the once-valued workers felt discarded, unwanted, with no sense that their stories ever mattered in the first place.

But stories always matter. Stories tell us who we are and how we got to where we are now. There are too many stories in Sheffield that have never been told. Yet so much time has passed now since the collapse of steel that there are fewer people around to tell the tale. Many of the 'Sheffield legends' of steel's finest years are no longer here, or no longer able, to tell their stories. So perhaps it is down to those of us who remember them to set the picture straight where we can, to tell the stories they can no longer tell for themselves.

This is one such story.

It is about life lived with an unsung hero of steel.

It is a turner's tale.

1

'We'll send for you when we want you, Frank...'

Back in the 1930s, before the war, and long before there was a National Health Service, doctors were few and cost money. Down in the old terraced streets of Pitsmoor, in the shadow of the steelworks, my Grandma Emily was the one people came to for help when they were sick. She had no training at all for this role as the local nurse; it was simply a matter of popular recognition. She was practical, dependable and, as my Dad remembered ruefully, very physically fit. 'She were a very energetic woman, my mother, strong as anything,' my Dad always used to say. 'When we were lads, good heavens, she got hold of you and you knew you'd been grabbed ...! There were no wriggling away when she grabbed you!' So she was always there whenever a woman went into labour, when a fever took a turn for the worse, or when someone was needed to lay out the dead. 'Run and get Emily!' was the first thing people thought of.

It was a tight-knit community my Grandma served. It had to be. Just the width of a road away from the blackened, towering walls of Firth Brown's steelworks, twelve back to back houses were jammed into a space not much bigger than an average couple of pre-war semis and their gardens. There was always something urgently needed in these families so crammed in together, always someone sending for Emily. Who Emily sent for when it was her turn, no-one ever said. My Dad was born in 1925 and named Frank, after his father, as was the way in those days. His brother, Ernest, came along three years later.

My Dad's whole childhood was spent across the road from the firm where he was to live out his entire working life. The little houses of Brightside Lane sheltered a community he always remembered with great affection. He loved to remember how all the children like himself would be 'racketing about' in the tiny yards after school, how people would talk for hours in the evenings, standing in little groups in the yards or sitting on doorsteps. 'When we were kids and we were sent to bed on summer nights you could hear them talking until it went dark,' my Dad would tell me, smiling at the memory.

My Dad's recollections of the 1930s were filled with all the nostalgia of a happy childhood, and my Grandma's memories were no less vivid. But there was precious little in her grown-up stories that would raise a smile. 'Nobody had a job. And nobody had any money.' That was what Grandma always said about the years before the war. It was not that nobody worked. What she meant was that nobody had a regular job. After the General Strike of 1926 the depression which settled upon the steel industry took away all hope of secure employment for most people. One or two men in a street, perhaps, would be in work, but only when they were sent for. My Granddad was one of these.

'You're a good worker, Frank, I'm sorry we've no more for you, you know how it is,' the foreman would say. So all the time my Dad was a boy, from the end of the 1920s right up until about 1938 when the likelihood of war brought back the demand for steel, his Dad never had steady work. Granddad worked as a press driver for Brown Bayley. They'd send for him to work maybe Monday and Tuesday, and then they'd say, 'we'll send for you again when we want you, Frank,' and it might be Wednesday and Thursday of the following week. Then maybe there would be three days the week after that, if he was lucky. And so it would go on, year after desperate year. Ironically, it took a World War with all the horrors of bombing, blackout and rationing to deliver the blessing of a living wage.

Still, they managed, as so many families did then, by scrimping and saving and going without. Granddad would trail up to the labour exchange on West Street in the centre of town to sign on when he had no work, but he would rarely get any financial assistance for his family. Usually this was because my Grandma was also finding work whenever she could. Emily was a file cutter. She was proud of that, proud of her skill at cutting the teeth in the file by hand. In those days, when there were no machines to turn out industrial files by the thousand, making files was considered a woman's job, because it was finicky work. The women would scratch grooves each way to make the teeth of the file, before the steel had hardened. So because Grandma had this occasional work, and it did only come along now and again, Granddad would be refused his two shillings at the National Assistance. However little unemployment benefits may be today, they were even less then, and the state's attitude towards would-be claimants was even more punitive.

'To get any kind of benefit,' my Grandma would say, 'you really had to have nothing'. She often told stories about people smuggling pots of jam from one house to another when the National Assistance inspectors appeared in the street. 'They would think nothing of searching the cellar heads looking for signs of good living. If you had a pot of jam you were obviously doing well, so you wouldn't get any assistance. They expected you to sell up virtually everything you had,' she would say. 'A table and chair would be acceptable, but a table and three chairs would be an extravagance and a chair or two would have to go to qualify as poverty.' The frustration this system created might sporadically boil over into public unrest, as my Dad recalled: 'The biggest amount of noise I ever heard was almost next door to where we were, where there was the Bessemer offices which used to belong to Firth Brown's and it were taken over to be used as an unemployment assistance board, giving out money. And I remember one day a huge crowd of unemployed coming down the road. The road was jam-packed with people outside the office.' But, as far as my Grandma was concerned, the biggest problem was that you didn't just have to be poor, you had to look poor as well. It was a very sore point with someone as proud and competent as Emily.

For the rest of her life my Grandma never got over her annoyance at the episode of the new shoes. My Dad attended All Saints, a school with fourteen classes, separate for boys and girls, fifty to a class. On one never-to-be-forgotten occasion, whilst he was still of primary age, they came to the school to hand out free shoes to the children of the local unemployed. My Dad turned up at home empty-handed and his mother promptly sent him back to get the much-needed help. 'Didn't you tell them your Dad was out of work?!' she'd demanded in astonishment. But, of course, he had done just that. He returned later, still with no shoes, but with a note from the teacher which read, 'Frank is always so neat and tidy, we didn't think he needed any.' He had always been sent off to school carefully and cleanly dressed with a little woolly tie, even if his jersey buttoned up to the neck. And this was the result. Grandma was still telling this story forty years later, not in pride at her own diligence and care, but in disgust at being cheated out of her entitlement.

However angry she was at this gross unfairness, or upset at her own poverty and the demeaning nature of the benefits system, none of it affected Grandma's politics. Times might be hard but she remained deeply patriotic with a profound love and respect for royalty. King and country were what mattered to her. And she was scarcely on her own in this. Whatever is sometimes assumed to the contrary, the Sheffield working class were not all committed socialists. When he was a lad, my Dad often liked to recall, politics was a very different business to the elections of today. For children in Sheffield's east end the democratic process became a seasonal street game, an excuse for a good scrap.

'There was always wild excitement down our way at the time of the local elections,' he remembered. 'Hundreds and hundreds and hundreds of people, men, women and children thronging the streets on election day. Kids used to thrash about – "who are you voting for?" and if you said t'wrong name you got a clip. All the lads used to walk about. You used to get your father, say, cause he were stronger than you, to get as much newspaper as he could and fold it up as tightly as he could and then tie string round it ever so tight, and it was then like a piece of wood 'cause it was hard. And then you'd have about two feet, three feet of string, which you'd wrap round your wrist, hold it in your hand and swing it round and ask people who they were voting for. You'd say "who do you vote for?" and if they said t' wrong name - bang! Or if you said t' wrong name, you'd get banged!'

Yet if election time was a time for the kids to let off steam it was still a fairly predictable business for the grown-ups, despite the attempts of Britain's own 1930s fascists, admirers of Hitler's Germany, to stir up some discontent. As my Dad recalled, 'The biggest excitement of course were when Oswald Mosley's stormtroopers came down, the blackshirts. And people were all shouting at 'em and there looked like being fights and so on, I remember there were always the police there. And they came down a number of times. Because I suppose they obviously thought there were easy pickings, people who were poor, they promised something, it'd sound like utopia, to get 'em to vote for 'em. I remember seeing 'em come down our road. But people were against 'em.'

It was a time when television, never mind the internet or social media, simply didn't exist and even newspapers would be few and far between, apart from the occasional 'Sporting Life' that people read for the horse racing. 'People were certainly less well-informed than they are today,' my Dad would say. 'And king and country, and t' prime minister were the thing. In areas like Pitsmoor you'd have thought the Labour Party would have been sailing but they weren't.' With no television and no tradition of journalists giving politicians a hard time, it was much more difficult to challenge the accepted order of things. 'Of course, you only ever heard politicians giving prepared speeches on the radio, sounding as if they knew everything. You never saw them on television like you do now, looking shifty. They used to return local Conservative councillors for a long, long while. It was tradition,' my Dad would say, summing the matter up. 'And not knowing any better,' he'd add, wryly, the ironic laughter playing around his eyes.

2

'I was never aware of it being bad...'

The world of Sheffield's east end in the 1930s seems to have been remarkably self-contained in its depression. When everyone you knew was in the same boat, of course, there were few grounds for feeling hard-done-by. As the powers-that-be were not rushing in to assist, there was nothing for it but to fend for yourself. So Grandma, with her strength and energy, and a determination which often bordered on obstinacy, was a natural leading light in the self-help that supported the community around the disturbingly quiet steelworks. Everyone knew her. Years later, when I walked down Spital Hill with her to go shopping, she would always be smart in her fitted coat and hat with their faint smell of mothballs, a modest brooch on her lapel. Everyone greeted her, and in the air around her always hung a sense of recognition of the natural dignity she had, of the standing she had earned in these Don Valley streets. As I trotted alongside her, what I felt and observed must have mirrored exactly my Dad's feelings about his own Grandma a generation earlier.

'Grandma Allott', as he always called her, was Welsh. She had arrived in Sheffield in the early 1890s as the wife of Frederick Allott and mother of a daughter, Mabel, who had been born in South Wales. With the usual vagueness of my family about its own history, no-one seemed to know, or care, what my Dad's grandfather, born and bred in Rotherham, had been doing in South Wales in the first place. Or even if he had ever been there. Nor was anyone very sure exactly where his Welsh wife hailed from. 'She was from Cardiff,' they would say. And then there would be a pause. 'Or was it Swansea?'

What everyone was sure of was that she was a bit of a cut above the rest of the family. Even her name, Margaret Rosina, told you that. A Welsh-speaking schoolteacher, stalwart of the local chapel, with a fine singing voice, a wearer of delicate gold-rimmed spectacles, the owner of a real silk paisley handkerchief; these were the things everyone remembered. 'I used to like my Grandma Allott because she thought I were marvellous,' my Dad remembered. 'She always called me Frankie, not Frank. She used to take me to the chapel on Attercliffe Common. She were a very tall lady, right nice-looking and striking. I were always proud to walk with my Grandma.' By the early 1920s she had the satisfaction of seeing her fourth son, my Granddad Frank, walking out with a girl who must have been remarkably like herself in character. Strong and dignified, upright and respectable, Emily must have been just the kind of daughter-in-law Margaret would have wanted. As times became much tougher, it must already have been obvious that it was going to take a lot more than a global economic depression to defeat a young woman who understood that certain standards had to be maintained.

So, as the 1930s ground on, my Grandma, Emily, did whatever she could to make ends meet. As well as the file cutting she used to go out cleaning, when she could get the work. Her most regular job was cleaning for Mr.Pearson, one of the teachers at the local school. She would clean usually half a day a week, but sometimes there would be the occasional extra. She often described how he once asked her to limewash a kitchen and a lavatory for a shilling. There wasn't any paint at the time, lime and water mixed to make a white was all that was available. And old Mr.Pearson gave her a shilling for limewashing his walls - 'I thought it was Christmas!' she used to say. It was certainly an event worth recounting twenty and thirty years later. There hadn't, after all, been many shillings about. Although, oddly enough, there was one member of the family who did have an unerring way of getting his hands on what there was.

My family were always great ones for respectability, it always seemed to me, as I was growing up. There were subjects that were never mentioned. There were events that were not to be discussed, certainly not in the presence of a child. Amongst the many little mysteries in our family which I was much too well-behaved to enquire about, Uncle George was the one who interested me most. 'He was a villain,' I would hear them say, but the voices would ring with affection. I can remember arriving at my grandparents' house one Saturday to find Grandma in tears, saying 'George has died'. Even then, I was not entirely clear whose brother he was and, observing the usual overriding discretion of my family, decided not to ask. It was years before I found out anything about him and, needless to say, he was scarcely a master criminal as it turned out.

In the early 1930s, when betting was illegal, my Grandma's brother, George, was the local unofficial bookie. He was well known in Pitsmoor as one of the local villains who used to fight in the streets. He was a tough man, 'tougher than anybody else', my Dad said. 'The police used to come down frequently and try to catch him bookmaking, to catch the men tossing - betting with the three coins, heads and tails and so on. The police knew him well because, when he wasn't bookmaking, they used to talk to him. It were allus "George" and whoever t'bobby was, first name terms. They were not deadly enemies, but they were there to catch him.'

Catching George was made a lot more difficult by the layout of the terraced streets with their interlinking 'double entries', passageways which would cut through from one street to another. If you knew what you were about, you could run down a passageway on, say, Forncett Street and come out in Carlisle Street and you'd only have run about fifty yards, maybe even less. The trouble was that, when so many were out of work, the stakes on the bets were more likely to be in copper than silver. George would run, pursued by the police, his pockets weighed down with heavy copper coins which he would sometimes be forced to fling out as he fled so that he could run faster. But there were plenty of opportunities for sanctuary: it was well understood around the district that George could go into any house when the police were in pursuit. If any likely door stood open George would dash in and then, of course, he was safe. The police were not allowed to follow him into a private house. People were on George's side, however much of a 'villain' he might have been, because they all knew him and, as my Dad put it, 'he used to be fairly philanthropic with his money, taking a man in for a glass of beer after he'd lost - well, it were their money anyhow!' And this system worked wonderfully well until somewhere around 1934 when George finally got three months in gaol for illegal gambling.

But what my Dad recalled most of all about George was a real child's memory - the wanton glittering of the coins in a time when coins were few and far between. 'Because he was the local bookie my Uncle George always had money when none of the other men did, because they were out of work. They never had any; he always did. And he used to come in to my Grandma's on Carlisle Street, his mother's, with his pockets full of money. And it'd only be - if there were a shilling or a sixpence, they'd be infrequent - it'd be pennies and twopences for betting in those days, coppers mainly. I'd perhaps be seven, I would think, and our Ernest'd be four, or something like that. And he used to put all his money on the table and he used to sit our Ernest in the middle of the table. Ernest'd throw money all over and my Grandmother'd be playing hell with my Uncle George for being daft with him.' This must be the only example of 'throwing money about' in the entire history of our family. George excepted, you can trace the generations of mattress stuffers and obsessive bill-payers, the scrupulous savers and penny-counters through an entire century. If this began to look ridiculous in a later age of credit cards, mortgages and bank loans, it was only because so many of us had never known, or had forgotten, the overwhelming fear of destitution which consumed them.

But in the world that the children inhabited the depth of deprivation of the 1930s was by no means obvious. There was no TV or websites to depict other lives, no glossy magazines, no adverts beguiling children into envious comparisons. Certainly, to my Dad and his pals, the acute anxieties of the adults around them might well appear as incidentals to the important issues in life. As he would remark, 'I was never aware of it being bad. It never occurred to me. I mean, as long as you could play football - though I do remember there being furious rows about the fact that I was always playing football and my shoe toes were hanging out: "Have you been playing football?!" my mother would shout at me. "No!!" I'd yell and run off. - As long as you could play at football and run in the house and get a slice of bread and jam and run out again, well, what more did you want?!' But it was no doubt a tribute to Grandma's skill at making do and to both my grandparents' talent for love and affection that a time of such shocking poverty could present a face of such security to a child.

When the steelworks finally started up in earnest just before the war their presence could be felt right through the house. My Grandma's mother had an ornament which, when the Bessemer hammer was working, would gradually make its way to the front of the mantlepiece and she would have to keep going up to it and pushing it back. At night, when they went to bed, she used to take it off the mantlepiece and put it on the floor to avoid finding it in pieces the next morning. Though it was not, of course, just the ornaments that could feel the force of the vibration from the Bessemer hammer as it boomed day and night across the road.

My Dad had a talent for drawing and painting right through primary school. It was his mother, Emily, who decided resolutely that nothing could be permitted to come of it, despite the intervention of All Saints' headmaster. 'Mester Spencer came and pleaded wi' me to let him go to art school', my Grandma would recall, still proud years later that her son had been so singled out. '"Frank's got talent," he said, "you've got to let him go." I said, "I can't, Mester Spencer, his Dad's out o' work."' Any money a lad could earn in those desperate years was crucial to a family's survival. There was no question of any art school for Frank, or of the grammar school where he had easily won a place. From their front door it was just a matter of walking across the road, maybe thirty yards, to be inside the factory. And so it was Emily who took him into the works in 1939 as soon as he turned fourteen. He left school on his fourteenth birthday on Good Friday and started his apprenticeship at Firth Brown on Easter Tuesday. It would be a full forty-four years later, through war and peace, boom and bust, before he was to leave this renowned Sheffield company to concentrate, at last, on his paintings in the garden shed.

3

'Too young for the first lot, too old for the second...!'

So, at the tender age of fourteen in 1939, the would-be artist was working a six-day, forty-eight-hour week at Firth Brown. Happily for my Dad it was not just a job that he was forced to do to earn money for his family, it was something which had already captured his imagination as a boy. He recalled how he had seen an exhibition of prop shafts and cranks made for the great ocean liner, the Queen Mary, in about 1934: 'that was my first spark of interest.' In the spring of 1939 he was earning a wage of eight shillings a week, with sixpence deducted for 'camp'. Skegness was to be the venue for this camp the apprentices were made to save up for, but my Dad never got there. 'It was Hitler's fault,' he used to say. He already had half a year as an apprentice turner behind him when war broke out and he was caught up in essential war work at once. Firth Brown's Machine Shops were producing armaments, from three inch diameter bore Bofors guns to sixteen inch diameter bore naval guns, torpedo warheads and armour plate for ships and tanks.

There was, doubtless, something about engineering which appealed to my Dad's love of precision. This was, after all, a young man who joined a carpentry class and who, by the time everyone else had constructed cupboards and tables, magazine racks and wicker stools, had produced a small but perfect square, to the bafflement of the tutor. As an apprentice turner, his first major contribution to the war effort was producing track pins. This was a job for which skilled men were paid three-halfpence for twelve, whilst apprentices got just three-eighths of a penny for the same number. By diligent and steadfast effort, this slight boy, who should have been sitting behind a grammar school desk if only his parents could have afforded it, managed unheard-of feats of production. By now he understood exactly how much his wages meant to his family and his hard work culminated in a week when he machined over 3000 track pins and managed to take home 'an extra 8/10d for my Mum. I was on top of the world!'

My Dad's war was spent machining by day and firewatching by night, stationed on the factory roof to spot wherever an enemy bomb might fall. By the time he was eighteen and of an age to enlist in the armed forces, he was already considered a skilled man. He had been hoping to drive a tank, but he was turned down. He would be far more use in the confines of Firth Brown producing the armaments essential for the war effort, he was disappointed to learn. Missing military service at the height of a war was an experience he and his father both shared. With the wisdom of hindsight, both of them were glad to have missed the bloodshed. '1898,' my Granddad used to say, 'that was the best year to be born. Two young for the first lot and too old for the second!' Though he wasn't, of course, too young for the First World War at all. It was simply that, like my Dad a generation later, the steelworks needed him more.

If it was steel that kept them both from seeing action on the battlefield, and may have saved their lives, it didn't stop them enjoying the pretence that they were just a pair of cowards. Whether it was an accusation they had faced in wartime from people who did not understand what a 'reserved occupation' was, I have no idea. But it was an issue they both invariably treated as a joke. My Dad would describe the certificate he had received at the end of the war for his services in the Home Guard: 'It said, "You were ready to lay down your life for King and Country" - nobody had ever mentioned that before. I was appalled!' A generation earlier, my Granddad did finally find himself in Belgium at the very end of the First World War. Once the military juggernaut had chewed up and spit out a generation of clerks and plumbers, farmworkers and bakers into the carnage of the trenches, it began in the end to demand that even the men who made the armaments take up their places in the line. Luckily for my Granddad, by the time he'd gone through basic training the armistice was in sight. 'What was it like?' I'd ask him, and he'd tell me about marching twenty-odd miles a day, carrying a pack, the scratchy uniforms and the sore feet. He wouldn't tell me what he saw. That was enough, in itself, to tell me that it was no laughing matter.

So the twentieth century's two world wars passed almost without comment from the men in my family. The most vivid tales belonged to the women and were those of the Home Front. My Mum, Joyce, was one of the now-celebrated 'Women of Steel', but she never saw it as a matter of pride. Far from it; she always saw herself as a thwarted secretary. Like my Dad, she had gained a place at grammar school but her family could not afford for her to go. As the next best thing she went at age fourteen to Bennett's College, combining work as a trainee clerk with classes in typing and shorthand. Any hope of a future as a secretary was scotched when her father came home from work one night and abruptly announced that he had got her a job at Simpkins sweet factory because it paid a shilling a week more. It was not the kind of decision you could argue with in those days. Soon after war broke out she received call-up papers directing her to report for duty in the steelworks. She was just sixteen and horrified at the news, but there was no arguing with the government either.

It might have seemed quite a leap to move from making sweets to making shells yet she rapidly learned how to turn metal at Firth Brown. But it was, literally, a baptism of fire. She was petrified of the machines, the belts whooshing up to the ceiling, the red-hot turnings flying out, cutting and burning skin. As a young teenager barely out of school she felt intimidated by the older men on the shop floor, of one in particular who clearly enjoyed her discomfort at his constant innuendo: 'I was forever landing on the same shift as him, worse luck! I used to dread it,' she remembered. Working nights, she would set off for her shift in the pitch dark of the blackout, walking briskly through the gigantic looming shapes of the steelworks, shovel in hand as a weapon, just in case. It was my Mum who gave me all my pictures of what the war was like: how she would find herself eating her tea on her own at the kitchen table at the end of a long day shift whilst everyone else, after an air raid warning, was already down the cellar. She described sitting for hour after hour feeling the vibration of the cellar steps, hearing the crashing of the bombs and then, the following morning, picking a route around the craters, the wrecked houses and mangled tramcars, to get back to work.

Perhaps it would have been different if I had ever known her father - even now I find it hard to think of him as my other Granddad - whose life, so bound up in the First World War, ended not long after the Second. He had joined the army as a lad and, because his father was a drayman and he had grown up with horses, had trained with the artillery at Hillsborough Barracks. In 1908 he had been sent to India to serve in the Royal Horse Artillery, working with the horses that pulled the gun carriages. When the First World War broke out, the India regiments were the first into France as the British Expeditionary Force, or what were dismissively called the 'contemptible little army'. From then on he was never out of action through all the major battles of the war. No doubt it was his position behind the guns which saved him for the London and North Eastern Railway once peace finally came. But he could not by then have been the same dapper young man as the one who stood so proudly in his dress uniform, foot resting on a tiger's skin, in the picture he sent home in 1910 from Mr.Dhanjeebhoy's photographic studio at Trimulcherry. Six years later, the plain sepia portrait of Corporal Wright tells a different story: a much older, almost middle-aged face, its faint smile betrayed by lines of strain about the eyes. The battles of Mons and Marne are behind him, the blood-soaked conflicts round Ypres are rolling relentlessly on.

What my Mum remembered of her father was the man who could never be serious, the tireless practical joker from whom even the local vicar was not safe. He was a man who would constantly hark back to his youth by making red hot curries and playing Indian music at full blast on Sunday mornings. He never spoke about the war, except to talk of the horses, and to express his pride in being one of the 'Old Contemptibles'. Year after year, he would drive his horse and dray for the railways until it was replaced by the newly-regulation lorry with the three-wheeled cab - his 'mechanical horse', he called it - and, year after year, he would carry the flag for the Old Contemptibles, marching through the city centre on Remembrance Day. His only reference to his wartime experiences came in his steadfast refusal to acquire an air-raid shelter once war broke out again in 1939. 'If it's got your name on it, that's it,' he'd say, defiantly standing out in the passage, watching as the bombs rained down.

As the Second World War was drawing to a close he would regularly come home from the railway with yet another home-made remedy someone had suggested for the gnawing pains in his stomach. That November he was already too sick, everyone thought, to go marching into town and stand in the cold by the cenotaph. But he insisted on going nonetheless and carrying the flag in the parade as always. Two months later the cancer had progressed through his liver, turning his body yellow, taking him away to the hospital with its short and rigid visiting times. 'It was different then. They didn't encourage you to stay,' my Mum said. But it was years before she told me the rest. 'They didn't get enough morphine. It wasn't like it is now. He used to cry out and shout with the pain and they had to take all his razor blades away from him.' After four years in the obscenity of the Flanders mud, even after a second world war of mind-numbing brutality, there were still, evidently, proper and improper ways to meet your maker from the confines of a hospital bed. In the years that followed, Mum and her family used to visit his grave to lay poppies for him on Remembrance Day, marking the man and his war all in one. It was not quite the same as simply taking flowers.

As for my Grandma, Emily, she carried on being a pillar of the community right through the war. She would queue for hour upon hour to fetch rations for elderly neighbours or people who were sick. Standing outside the butcher's and the grocer's on Spital Hill, she braved the freezing cold through every winter of the war, and beyond into the sparseness of peacetime, until rationing finally ended almost a decade later. It was an endurance test which was the source, she was convinced, of the arthritis which crippled her old age. My Mum always remembered how it was Grandma, rather than her own stepmother, who had queued endlessly for every single ingredient for the wedding cake and the tea when she and Dad got married three years after the end of the war.

My parents, Joyce and Frank, met at Firth Brown in 1943 when they were both eighteen. They got engaged not long after the war in Europe ended, in the summer of 1945, but the wedding had to wait. Much to my Dad's disgust, he was promptly called up as soon as the war was over. He joined the RAF, looking forward to the chance to become a pilot, only to find he stood little chance of getting airborne. After basic training, he was dispatched to Caister Camp in Lincolnshire to help ensure the safety of the realm from some of its many prisoners of war. In what he took to be the characteristic failure of the RAF to see beyond the officer class there was no recognition of his natural sharpness and near-perfect coordination. He would almost certainly have made a brilliant pilot. But he only went up in a plane once during his entire period of duty.

Still, National Service had its uses, not least in supplementing the meagre post-war rations to take home to my Grandma. As a child, I remember listening to Dad's tales of catching rabbits in the woods around the camp. I thought at the time that he was seriously describing basic butchery skills. 'What you do, you see, when you want to clean a rabbit, is you draw a line down its middle with a knife, then you pick it up and whirl it round your head as fast as you can,' my Dad would say, with a huge grin. 'This is why all t'trees in Lincolnshire are covered in bits o' rabbits' innards, hanging down like Christmas decorations!' 'Oh, Frank, stop it!' my Grandma would exclaim, covering her ears and walking off into the kitchen. National Service in post-war Lincolnshire was scarcely the stuff a young man's dreams of adventure were made of. Yet, oddly enough, it offered, in the end, a glimpse into another world altogether in a way which was to have a profound effect on the lives of both my Dad and me.

4

'Adolf Hitler? Never heard of him…!

'At ease, men.'

The boots clomped on the wooden hut floor. 'Now, as you know,' the commanding officer intoned, 'the RAF has charge of all of this camp and, with it, a significant number of German Prisoners of War. We have received instructions that all of these men have to be released and sent back to Germany in due course. But only when it is safe to do so. Some of these prisoners are dangerous Nazis. But some, we believe, are young men who have no Nazi sympathies at all and were simply caught up in the events of the war.'

The row of recently-conscripted aircraftsmen stared into the middle-distance, uneasily, wondering what was coming next. 'There will be three waves of release of POWs,' their commanding officer continued. 'In accordance with the instructions we have received from above, those least implicated in recent events in Germany will be designated 'White' and released in the near future. Those about whom we are more concerned will be designated 'Grey' and released at some date yet to be determined. Those who were fully involved in the activities of the Third Reich will be designated 'Black' and will, of course, be detained for the longest period of time. What we have to do now is determine which of these Prisoners of War falls into which category.'

The conscripts tried not to catch the officer's eye. Someone, clearly, was about to be given an impossible job. 'You and you, step forward,' the command rang out. 'It will be your job to find out who the Nazis are.' My Dad and his mate, two lowly conscripts barely past their basic training, occupied in supervising prisoners' farm work in post-war Lincolnshire, rolled up their sleeves.

'We worked out a list of serious questions to ask them all,' my Dad recounted. 'Had they ever been a member of the Nazi Party? Had they been in the Hitler Youth? Things like that. We interviewed dozens and dozens of them and we got the same answers every time - "Adolf Hitler? Never heard of him!" We went back to the commanding officer and said we couldn't prove that any of them had been Nazis. But that wasn't the right answer because the government had decided that they had to be divided into three groups and released in three lots. They just sent us back out again with instructions to try harder.'

At this point in the story, my Dad would invariably start laughing. 'We didn't know what to do. Then I had an idea. "What we'll do", I said, "is look for those with the most English-sounding names, like Braun and Schmidt, and they can be 'White'. And the ones with the most Germanic-sounding names, like Schickelgruber, can be the Nazis." They had no chance. So we went out onto the square and all the POWs were lined up and we read out the names of the 'Whites', 'Greys' and 'Blacks'. There was uproar! Oh dear, everybody was throwing up their hands in horror, demanding to see the officers. The officers, of course, insisted a thorough investigation had been carried out in the best traditions of British Intelligence. So there wasn't a thing they could do about it.'

This, I think, was my introduction to the notion that what we read in history books may not be what actually happened. Or that what we think we are looking at may not bear any relation to what is actually going on behind the scenes. Over the years I have read numerous descriptions of the painstaking, intelligence-led process of de-Nazification carried out by UK security personnel at the end of the war. They always make me smile. It was one of my earliest lessons in understanding that people can be endlessly inventive in getting round official instructions. My Dad was always happy to underline the point of the story: 'never believe everything they tell you, Susan!'

However unpromising the beginning of military service might have been, it soon became unexpectedly enjoyable and memorable. For the biggest surprise to my Dad was the discovery that many of the German prisoners were young lads very like himself. He very soon struck up a friendship with two of them in particular. 'We were so similar,' he would always say, 'the sense of humour was just the same.' They were soon inviting him along to their film shows, screenings of the original German versions of classics such as 'The Land of Smiles'. My Dad had always loved the music of films and operettas, so he was only too delighted to enjoy these German musicals, especially when they starred Richard Tauber, one of his favourite tenors.

Seeing his interest in their film shows and enjoying his company, the German lads were soon offering to teach him the language. He didn't take them up on it and regretted it ever afterwards when he realised that he would have enjoyed language learning. 'I was too young and stupid,' he would say, ruefully. Given their English-sounding surnames, his two friends must have been amongst the first to be allowed home. He was touched when they presented him with a parting gift they had made themselves, intending it to be given to Joyce, his bride-to-be. It was a beautiful marquetry photograph holder with frames for two photos arranged either side of a carved wooden heart. I have it now and on the base it reads, in pencil, 'German POWs, Caister Camp 1946, Weber, Weitze', in my Dad's unmistakable, flamboyant hand.

The photo frame was not the only thing the German lads left behind them. The friendships he had formed changed my Dad's attitudes forever. He had just spent six years, the whole of his teenage life, making artillery shells to be fired at Germans and watching at night for the bombs they were dropping on us. Then, when the nightmare ended, he came face to face with lads whose lives had been much the same as his. Even as the full extent of the

Nazis' atrocities was being revealed to a horrified world, my Dad was discovering that these young men were just as appalled as he was at the crimes committed in their name. Like him, they had had no influence on events and had played the part they had been made to play. Though my Dad's war never took him further than Lincolnshire it brought unexpected revelations about the realities behind the international headlines. What he learned at Caister Camp was to influence his beliefs and his actions for the whole of the rest of his life. As the years went by he was appalled and disgusted that, even after two World Wars, the threat of war had not receded. He was always one for pithy comments and never made speeches, but his words on the subject were a regular refrain in our house as I grew up: 'People don't want war. It's politicians that want war. It's all about power and greed. Look where it gets you.'

After the RAF, my Dad returned to his job as a machinist at Firth Brown in 1947. It was a time of tremendous upheaval as the firm coped with the transition from wartime to peacetime needs. For the rest of his life, my Dad kept his 'Fowler's Mechanics' and Machinists' Pocket Book 1948' with its fine-printed pages of technical data and procedures. Just a glance at this well-thumbed 'Synopsis of Practical Rules for Fitters, Turners, Millwrights, Erectors, Pattern Makers, Foundrymen, Draughtsmen, Apprentices, Students, Etc., Etc.', made it plain that the impact of World War was still far from absorbed. Even three years after the end of hostilities, the numerous advertisements which graced its pages came with a disclaimer that 'owing to war conditions' goods made of raw materials were 'not necessarily available for export'. As the country began to pick itself up after six years of total war, my Dad was once more hard at work developing his skills on the varied production of the Light Machine Shop. It was the beginning of what he would later always describe as 'thirty years of boom' for Firth Brown, and indeed for the whole of Sheffield steel.

5

'Tea, Oswald...?'

It was in 1948 that the long-awaited wedding finally took place. My parents, Frank and Joyce, set up home in rented rooms on Petre Street next door to the house my grandparents had moved to some time before. As my Dad commented, 'in those days the height of people's ambitions was not only to live on the same street as their mother, but if they got in the same yard as their mother they'd made it then! Not like you!' he'd usually add, pointedly. Once the fear and austerity of wartime was behind them young people who had had to grow up very fast could suddenly allow themselves to have a bit of fun. Both my parents loved to sing and Ellesmere offered the perfect outlet for their talents. On the hill above the steelworks, just down the road from their new home, an entire troupe of young men and women staged musicals, long forgotten now, like 'The Country Girl' and 'The Chocolate Soldier', or popular plays such as J.B.Priestley's 'When We Are Married'.

The curling black and white photographs from the Ellesmere productions show my Dad every inch the leading man in black tie and tails or in naval uniform, the east end lad making a more-than-passable toff. Years later this still amused him and he would quote odd bits of his performances at appropriate moments as a kind of running gag. 'Tea, Oswald?' he'd say at mealtimes in a light, ultra-posh voice, turning his arms into a teapot handle and spout. All my immediate family seemed to have been involved in the Ellesmere shows: there's a snap of my Mum looking coy in a long satin evening gown, or another where she's holding aloft a tambourine in the gypsy chorus. And there's Mum's sister, my Aunt Margaret - she's the gypsy with the glasses. But it was my

Dad with his fine tenor voice who took the leading roles, evidently with some conviction. His cousin, Sandra, recalled how at the age of twelve she had been taken along to one of these shows and had been aghast to see him kiss the leading lady. 'He can't do that,' she had yelled from the stalls, 'he's married to Joyce!'

After my grandparents moved to Petre Street their grown-up and growing family still gathered around them. Three houses with brown-painted doors shared a yard, one facing out and the other two facing inwards. Grandma and Granddad had one of these and, in the other, lived Mrs.Priestley. My parents rented rooms in Pee Pee's house, as I always called her before I could get my tongue round four syllables. Meanwhile, my Uncle Ernest, Dad's brother, and my Auntie Ivy rented the front of my grandparents' house. From my point of view, this was an entirely happy proximity which allowed me to race between four sets of people at will, flinging doors wide open as I ran. Each little household would attempt, usually unsuccessfully, to lure me into eating a proper meal. One of the newest little family mysteries in these pre-slum-clearance years I had invented all by myself. A tendency to be ill at every opportunity and a determination to avoid food at all costs had my parents constantly waging war with me over vitamins, cod liver oil and thick clinic orange juice, or dragging me on the tram up to the clinic for sun ray treatment and anxious weighing sessions. Ernest and Ivy would inform on my rapid progress round their bit of the house, 'She's had four beans and a chip,' they would say, and I would escape into Pee Pee's, ignoring the despairing glances and resigned shrugs which passed between them all.

The bells always gave me a good chance to get out of food's way. I loved to listen whenever they rang out, which seemed to be nearly every day. All Saints Church towered above us on the hill which loomed behind the wall, behind the lavatories at the end of the yard. There were no proper gardens on Petre Street. Stone flags covered the yard as far as the steps and the asphalt slope that led to the lavatories. A little patch of ground, lovingly edged in lobelia and allysum, held a couple of grime-covered rose bushes against the lavatory wall. All Saints' immense black-pointed steeple reared over us, the bells cascading down onto the slate roofs, reverberating around the little yards all along the top of Petre Street. The steeple could be seen from way across the valley, over the tops of the factory chimneys and the great black mass of the machine shops which still bore the names of their Victorian partner-founders. Firth Brown, Brown Bayley, Balfour Darwin, Firth Vickers: these were the names I grew up with. It was John Brown who had built the church, concerned, like so many paternalistic entrepreneurs of the Victorian era, for the spiritual health and sobriety of his workforce. In the mid-nineteenth century men from the ranks of terraced houses packed upon this hillside above their places of work would throng the Bible study classes at All Saints. A hundred years later the pubs and the betting shops had resoundingly won the battle for men's minds but All Saints continued to perform its duties for the parish. Saturday after Saturday, Grandma would take me round to its gates to watch the weddings come and go beside a little huddle of grannies and their charges, oohing and aahing at the lemon and pink taffeta of the bridesmaids' dresses, the swoosh of their paper nylon underskirts.

My grandparents' living room was always dark, overshadowed as it was by the hillside walls and the steeple of All Saints, so the fire would be lit almost all year round. Definitely all year, if my Granddad had his way. He always felt the cold. The fire took pride of place in the centre of the enormous cast iron range which dominated one side of the room. Granddad would pile huge lumps of coal into the grate, whacking them with the poker to make the sparks fly out and the flames shoot high up the chimney. 'That's a nice little blaze,' he'd say, watching my Grandma leave the room and eyeing the thermometer with satisfaction. Sometimes he'd make a show of examining the temperature at close quarters and murmur, 'I think we'll just have another couple of degrees', and the coal would pile on and the poker would come out. My Grandma, meanwhile, would stand in the kitchen with the door wide open to the yard, fanning her face with the skirt of her apron, huffing and puffing. This little war of attrition between them, and the many jokes it entailed, went on for decades. The fire-stoking would always get worse, as Grandma well knew, whenever she went out, followed by a frenzy of damping-down at her imminent return. She would come in, exclaiming at the wall of heat which hit her, to see my Granddad, innocent-eyed, on his chair next to the fire in his jumper with his cardigan well buttoned-up.

When I was a toddler, Granddad would sit me on a stool right next to the range until my legs turned mottled from the heat, whereupon he'd turn me round to face the other way with an 'are you done yet?', like a roast on a spit. I thought this was great fun then but, as I got older, I went over to Grandma's camp, ending up right out in the yard, blowing cold breaths onto my face, listening to the peeling bells. By the time I was old enough to enjoy my grandparents' tussles with the thermometer, we no longer lived on Petre Street. When I was two our names reached the top of the council house waiting list and, suddenly, we were off to what really were pastures new.

6

'Time and commotion...'

By the time we were living in our smart new council house on Gleadless Valley my Dad had an unexpected new job to go with it. He had clearly never been destined for an office job and it is debatable whether, in the normal course of events, he would ever have made such a move. But events, as they are prone to do, took a sudden and unpleasant turn. My Dad's best friend at Firth Brown was Ken Bliss. They were apprentices together, a pair of bright lads, getting on, doing all right, enjoying a glass of beer together after work. One day they were coming back into work after lunch, crossing the yard with its railway tracks in and out of the machine shops. As a train began to move out, my Dad nipped across the line and Ken followed him over. He was not quite fast enough. One of the wagons caught him and crushed his leg. It had to be amputated. Ken's working life as a machinist was over and my father was overcome with guilt at the moment of miscalculated risk which had left him unscathed and caused such grievous injury to his friend. I don't think he ever got over it. Standing outside our house one night, years later, when Ken came over I remember the troubled expression on my Dad's face as his friend struggled to get out of his adapted car.

Ken himself never blamed my Dad for the accident and they remained firm friends. Thereafter, their careers took on a curious symmetry as they worked their way up the ladder. But the first rung was Ken's transfer onto a desk job into which my Dad duly followed him. The firm and the unions had agreed that, in return for better rates of pay, a new system of payment would be put into the Machine Shops based on a more sophisticated measurement of

Work Study. For the first time stop watches were to be accepted on the shop floor. So my Dad was asked to join a team of three to implement the new system and sent on a series of courses to prepare for this job. As he wrote much later, 'Our system was to be Time and Motion study and, in view of the rapidly escalating friction between the Study team and the Shop Floor, quickly became known as Time and Commotion. Part of the agreement between unions and management was that "Operators should assist in setting the new allowed times". In some cases this was done, in others some operators gave us every assistance possible, short of actually helping. In view of the fact that many well-established times for the many different operations were reduced by ten or fifty percent without a corresponding increase in pay, perhaps this was not surprising.'

As these comments suggest rate-fixing was not an easy business. It was not just the maths, though that was tricky enough, working out machine speeds and machining times in order to set the rate for every individual job the men were working on. It was what happened when the calculations were complete that made the job so tough. However fair the rate-fixer tried to be, the answer, of course, was never enough as far as a machinist was concerned. The ensuing tussles, arguments and out-and-out shouting matches were an exhausting way to spend a working day. As my Dad would recall, 'if a machine operator wished to use what is called industrial language he would do so, and many frequently did. You'd got immense power and absolutely no authority.' Once a year without fail the lid would come off. The head of the rate-fixing section, someone my Dad invariably referred to at home with great affection as 'old Butler', would take his proteges, my Dad, Ken Bliss and their other lifelong friend, Jack Howard, down to a pub in the Wicker on Christmas Eve. After lunchtime hours with the doors firmly locked, 'old Butler' would prevail upon his friend who ran the place to pour rum into pint pots.

One of my earliest childhood memories is of my Mum's increasingly frantic clock-watching one Christmas Eve when my Dad failed to appear. Some time in the middle of the evening he lurched into view through the kitchen door, looking a little less dapper than usual, and proceeded to ricochet off the living room wall and the shelving opposite, career around my toys in the middle of the floor and set off upstairs without saying a word. My mother went up behind him and I was left on the carpet listening to the mysterious crashes and bangs above my head as he attempted to get into bed. 'What's the matter with Dad, Mum?' I asked helpfully when she came back downstairs. 'He's just having a sleep,' she said, with that teeth-clenched outrage which is guaranteed to follow dread. The next day he confessed the reason for his lateness: he had felt so ill on the bus weaving its way up to Gleadless Valley that he had got off several stops before the terminus and fallen asleep in the snow on a pitch-black hillside half an hour from home. To the end of his life, even after all the huge responsibilities he was to shoulder in later years, he still called rate-fixing 'by far the most difficult job I have ever done.' Yet the experience and skill it gave him spawned an interest in issues of efficiency and performance-related pay which was to stay with him throughout his working life and beyond.

7

'It's fresh air, Susan, you're not used to it...'

After Petre Street, Gleadless Valley was a shock to the system. It could not have been more different from the dark and filthy streets of Pitsmoor. The steelworks made the wealth of the city and provided the work in which so many took pride but all this came at a cost. Effluent from the factories poisoned the river and thick black smoke poured continually out of hundreds of chimneys over the houses the length of the Don Valley. When the sun shone through the windows the dust in the air glittered with microscopic pieces of metal. This was the state of the air people were breathing. Having a 'bad chest', which often meant chronic bronchitis, was a regular complaint on the steep hills above the steelworks. At its worst, in a bad winter, chemists would dispense surgical masks to guard against the killer smogs. Like most men at that time my Granddad was a smoker but he stopped in the space of a day after one never-to-be forgotten night of smog. Walking home up the hill from the works he had suddenly found himself gasping for breath, on his hands and knees, barely able to see a yard in front of himself for the filth in the freezing November air. If he couldn't do a thing about the pollution in which he spent his life at least he could throw away the 'Park Drive' cigarettes.

We arrived on Gleadless Valley in mid-winter, one of the first families to move in. The estate was so new that very few houses had yet been built. Our street seemed to stand in grand isolation in an immense field of snow as far as the eye could see. As the removal van drove off it felt as if we had been deposited in the icy wastes of Siberia. The reaction of my two-year-old self to all of this passed into family legend. Years later my parents would still enjoy describing how I promptly sat down on a suitcase and announced, 'I'm not stopping here!'

It didn't take long for me to change my tune. Or for my parents to feel the benefit of the change, despite the lack of shops or amenities and the long trek into town. When spring came we were transported to a different world of nature, colour, wildlife and open land. Like a miracle, we suddenly found ourselves in the countryside. Not only were we right on the farthest edge of the city but the whole estate as it developed was designed to give a sense of space. It was 'Mediterranean-style', the council proudly told us and on summer days that really didn't seem too far-fetched. There were pathways, gennels and squares between the houses, grass growing everywhere and panoramic views over the wooded hillsides tumbling down towards a city centre still often hidden in smoke and fog. At a time when few people owned a car, it was one huge and glorious playground for children.

There had been so little to look at in the leafless streets of Pitsmoor where even the sky so often seemed daubed in grime. Down in the bottom of the Don Valley the works rose in sheer walls of blackened brick or dark corrugated iron, mile after mile beside the filth of the river. 'When I get down there I often think it's like going into Grand Canyon - these huge walls rising up either side of you,' my Dad would always say once we had moved to our hilltop world at Gleadless. For up on Gleadless Valley it was a different story. Two hundred yards from our house stood a sign which bore the incredible word 'Derbyshire'. Past the sign there were fields, trees and farms with cows, horses, sheep and, of course, huge, decaying heaps of manure. 'What's that funny smell, Dad?' I'd say as we strolled past. 'It's fresh air, Susan, you're not used to it,' he'd laugh.

As our new estate sprang up, everything was shiny bright. The doors were painted different primary colours on different streets: Landseer was blue, Orpen was yellow, Gibbons was green, Constable was red, Raeburn was purple. The street names themselves, an array of nineteenth-century British artists, reflected a typical post-war reforming zeal to bring culture to the masses. Far away from the dark-brown, dark-green and mushroom paint and the donkey-stoned steps of Pitsmoor, proud young fathers did DIY and produced rosebeds and small neat lawns as if in permanent competition. 'Who do you think's got the best garden on this street?' Dad once asked. 'Mr. Webber,' I said, stupidly, because he had the end wall so could grow climbing roses. Dad's expression made it clear that I could do a lot better than that. After that, I always awarded top marks to our house.

It was bright in our house. It was a true 1950s world. All the lovely colours were inside as well as out. My Mum spent endless happy hours choosing wallpaper from the huge collection of books at Blaskeys in town and then enjoyed all the cutting and pasting to match the patterns perfectly on our walls. There were orange fish blowing bubbles all the way up the kitchen walls, there were pink roses in the living room, there were grey and chesnut horses all around my bedroom. On the landing upstairs Dad painted each door a different brilliant colour, just like the doors on the streets. It was lovely. Sometimes I would just sit on my bed with the door open enjoying first the yellow, then the red, then the blue. We were very up-to-date.

Colour seemed to be everywhere, suddenly, then. When we first moved up there Mum would take me down to meet Dad coming home from work at the bus stop near to Lightwood Lane. I'd be watching for Dad but, as he got off the bus, I'd have a smile for him and half an eye on the amazing luminous pink and green socks of the teddy boys swarming past me up the gennel. I had bright clothes too: a red bonnet and coat with a black velvet collar, or an orange coat that my Mum had knitted with skirts that swirled out when I went racing down the street and round the corner to find my friends. Whenever we went back to Pitsmoor I felt like a jewel-bright butterfly landing briefly on a discarded chrysalis of smoke-blackened brick.

After we left for the distant vistas of Gleadless Valley and ever more council houses were built, the terraces of Pitsmoor became a lot less crowded. Suddenly there were fewer and fewer young families living in 'rooms'. It left my grandparents' house with a curiously lopsided feel about it. It was as if they expected the family back at any moment so they never got into the habit of using all of it again. This would not have seemed so odd but for the fact that the unused and unloved 'front room' was the only place with natural sunlight. After Uncle Ernest and Auntie Ivy moved out into a house of their own, round the corner from the church on Sedan Street, I can't remember ever sitting there. It became a repository for fancy things: the pastel-coloured, luminous cups and saucers brought back from Blackpool which had a high shelf all to themselves, the silver-paper pictures of a Dutch boy and girl, the dark-framed portrait over the unlit hearth. 'Who do you think that is?' Grandma had asked me once when I was very small, pointing at the young person with scraped-back hair photographed in 1916. 'Is it Granddad?' I had asked, hopefully. 'No, it's me!' she had laughed, in mock outrage that I didn't recognise her. But it seemed to me an understandable mistake, seeing as I had never set eyes on Granddad when he had any hair.

Saturday always saw us back in the dark Pitsmoor streets visiting Grandma and Granddad. Whenever we turned up, we would let ourselves in through the unlocked front door, calling out 'hello!' as we trooped past the neat brown armchairs and the bright sun-speckled carpet beneath the window nets to get into the familiar darkness beyond. The sole exception to this rule was when I went with Granddad to add silver paper, little bits of purple, green and gold chocolate wrappings, to his collecting bag which he would take down to 'The Crown' when it was full to put towards a guide dog. And then it would be straight back to 'the house' with its heavy furniture, the dark green, velvety, tassled cloth on the wooden table and, above all, the comfort of Granddad's roaring fire in the centre of the huge cast-iron range.

8

'She always managed to make a shilling do two shillings-worth of work...'

For me, and for my beloved Granddad, Saturday had far more to it than this. Saturday was racing day. And my Granddad was a racing man. Not that he ever actually went to the races in his life, as far as I'm aware. But every Saturday he would settle his trilby on the bald dome of his head and walk down Spital Hill to put on a shilling here or there at Lishman's. We used to pass Lishman's on our way home from Pitsmoor on the bus: a single door huddled intriguingly at the foot of the colossal blackened brickwork of the Wicker Arches, the railway bridge which heralded the beginning of 'town', or the start of the miles of steelworks down Saville Street, depending on which way you were going. Above Lishman's doorway was a single panel with a chesnut horse and jockey galloping endlessly against a blue-tiled background. I always had to make sure that I caught sight of the horse on my way home; it was one of the landmarks which brightened the endless two-bus journey out to Gleadless Valley. Lishman's horse, the pet shop in the Wicker with the aquarium in the window, Woolworths' gold and red lettering, the blue flashes of the tram-line junctions in Fitzalan Square: all these had to be noted and ticked off the list on the first half of the journey home.

Granddad loved the racing but he was never a gambler. He was far too much of the responsible family man to put more than a bob or two on every Saturday. We would arrive at Grandma and Granddad's dark brick terrace in time for the racing and Granddad would sit me on the little wicker stool in front of what seemed then the big black and white screen with instructions to 'shout for my horse, Susan'. And I would sit there, dutifully yelling as the horses came up the straight to the winning post. If it came nowhere he'd call it a 'scrubbing brush', but if it won it would be a 'good 'un'.

'Are you going to fetch your winnings, Granddad?'

'Not yet,' he'd say, cagily. 'There's another race to watch.'

Grandma would groan. Another double, or treble, or accumulator. Lots of opportunities not to pick up any winnings again. By the end of the afternoon, Lishman's was usually a bob or two richer and I'd got a few more names to add to my mental collection of 'good 'uns' and 'scrubbing brushes'. But Granddad made sure I knew that he thought proper betting was a mug's game, that money was something to be looked after carefully, saved up in my red-pillar-box money bank and converted into non-winning premium bonds. At least, that way, the money only disappeared gradually through the constant nibbling of inflation.

Our family didn't do credit, or hire purchase as it was known then, it saved up. And if it couldn't afford things it went without or it waited, patiently. When I was very small I could never understand why, long before birthdays and Christmas, Grandma would be telling my Mum, 'I've laid away a little frock for her on Spital Hill.' She would set off each week for the small shop with its dark wooden counters and its Aladdin's Cave of children's clothes piled and hung from floor to ceiling to knock a bit more silver or coppers off the total carefully noted in the ledger. It would take months for her to pay it all off and the big day would arrive when she could take the dress away with her. Laying things away and carefully sorting money into different purses and boxes and insurance books was how she 'always managed to make a shilling do two shillings-worth of work,' as my Dad put it. No-one in my family liked risk: they were too used to having nothing to contemplate losing any of it. So the racing, for me, was a spectator sport only. Over the years, my growing ability to pick long-shot winners could be guaranteed to disappear if it ever actually involved money.

Sometimes, when I was still quite small, I would go and stay with Grandma and Granddad so that my parents could go out at weekends. I loved these special times in their house when it was just them and me. Grandma took charge. There would be cheese and beetroot sandwiches for tea in slabs of bread which she'd cut cockeyed from a large white loaf. She would stand the loaf upright and saw the breadknife towards herself, but no matter how straight the slices looked she would always end up with a triangular heel of bread instead of a crust. As she saw this happening she never seemed to be able to even the slices up and she would stand there, saying, 'look what I've done with this!', her ample sides heaving in silent laughter. There were always lots of cups of tea, biscuits from the caddy and, of course, home-made apple pie on her treasured fluted plates.

At night I would sleep in Grandma's bed with Granddad banished to the small and cold front bedroom where nobody ever slept and where, in the morning, he would show me cowrie shells amongst the glass ornaments on the dressing table and put them to my ear. 'Listen,' he'd say, 'you can hear Blackpool. And this one is Cleethorpes,' cupping the second shell to the other side of my head. And I would marvel at how the shells transmitted the sea from one side of the country to the other. In the bedroom with Grandma it always seemed warm from the heat of the fire beneath us. The bed would rumble as she sat on the edge to roll off her stockings and unbutton her enormous pink corsets. As she settled down under the covers I would snuggle up and be astonished to see her face suddenly shrunken and her toothless smile.

Yet, even at moments like this, with Grandma you somehow never lost sight of how strong she was. To this day I remember the strength of her hands as she donkey-stoned the front step and black-leaded the range, as she rubbed the huge green block of Fairy soap onto wet cloths or lifted mounds of washing through the ringer. However reluctantly and incompetently I clean my own house now I find it impossible not to think of her and her methodical, powerful strokes of the brush or mop whenever I attempt the same. Whilst I remember Granddad for his laughter and his playfulness, his whimsical behaviour and funny sayings, she remains in my mind like a rock, like resolution embodied. You couldn't imagine anything powerful enough to wear her down. And, indeed, nothing ever did until the mid-1970s when, after ten years of happy retirement, my Granddad suddenly died. She seemed, overnight, to shrink down inside her pinny and her cardigan, felled by the hammer blow of his loss. After half a century of loving partnership, she was at sea. It was only then we realised how much of her strength had come from him.

9

'Make sure you don't ever stop looking...'

Both my Mum and Dad had always talked to me, endlessly, since I could first understand, though in the pre-school years it's Mum I remember the most. She would play the radio ('It's Bernard Hermann and the Northern Dance Orchestra!') or a record of one of her favourite singers with hits from the top musical shows and we would join in together, laughing, as we tried to learn the words. But with my Dad there was often a mysterious sense of being in training for some large but unspecified task. Like the thwarted artist he was, he insisted on making me look at things. 'You'd be amazed how many people never look up when they're walking down the street. They don't know what the buildings look like, they only see the shop fronts. If you look up, you see so many interesting things.' We'd specialise in looking when we were out of town as well, on our walks past the 'Derbyshire' sign. There would be squirrels scampering through ivy up the ancient sycamores, blackbirds shrieking out a warning of our approach, crows circling in anticipation over the decaying smells of the farmyard.

However bright the houses of Gleadless Valley seemed after the dark terraces of Pitsmoor the best colours and the best looking were always to be had down Lightwood Lane, especially when the weather had done its worst. Dressed up like Rupert Bear in warm check trousers and wrap-around scarf I would trek down there hand-in-hand with Dad in the massive snows of 1963, seeing how far into the drifts we could stand in our wellingtons. The woodland world, turned white, revealed motorways of traffic by rabbits' paws and squirrels' feet, by the hop of sparrows and the run of starlings. Under the trees where the lichen glowed lime-green in the January sun, the snow lay blue and purple or, suddenly, blindingly white where crystal shards caught a pallid, dying gleam. There was never anyone in this winter world but us, trudging our familiar circuit on unfamiliar crackling ground, back round to Oaks Park, past the Bagshawe Arms and home to the heady smell of Yorkshire pudding and gravy.

Only once, as I recall, did the woods attract tourists, and that was in the days after the 1962 tornado which mysteriously flattened swathes of Sheffield and left the rest of the country unmoved and uncomprehending. After the livid bruise of the sky had returned to its everyday blue and grey, after the flattened prefab houses were no longer the stars of the regional TV news, there were the trees down Lightwood Lane, tortured and groaning with their roots upturned. It was impossible to follow our usual path. We took great detours around vast oaks and beeches, their branches spanning across the rich black earth where the bluebells would spring, their roots ripped upright, higher than a man. It was eerie and strange to see the devastation wrought in a night, to see the wood brought low. In time, the helpless trunks were cleared and the hollows grew over with ivy and saplings. But it sometimes made me cry to see how the wood was hurt and wonder how the great trees, so solid for decades, for centuries, could be lost in a calamity so unforeseen. 'Nothing can last forever, Susan,' Dad said, fumbling for a handkerchief for my dripping nose. 'Everything and everybody has to die some day. But there's always something new comes in its place. There's always some good, in the end, comes out of every bad thing that happens. You just have to look for it. Make sure you don't ever stop looking.'

And I didn't. Because wherever we were, he was forever teaching me things, asking me to work things out and, as time went on, deliberately arguing with my opinions to make me think. He was constantly pushing my intellectual curiosity, encouraging me to dig a bit deeper and asking me to justify the things I was saying. It was just not typical in those days when people thought girls were not as smart as boys and didn't deserve the same education. As I grew into adolescence it became very clear to me that the other girls I knew had not been treated like this. But the most important example of this took place when I was just six years old and was destined to have a huge impact on the rest of my life.

One night my Dad came home from work with a tin globe he had bought for me in Woolworths. He had decided it was time to learn about other countries. He took it out of its bag, stood it on the table and set it dizzily spinning. My amazement at what I saw made me stop the globe with my finger on an enormous orange expanse that seemed to wrap itself right around the northern hemisphere: 'what's that?!' 'That's Russia,' he said. And the questions were forming themselves at once: how could anywhere be so huge? Why had the other countries let anywhere get so large? If it was the biggest, was it the strongest? On the tin globe the endlessly diverse countries of Europe huddled together in a space the size of - well, nothing much, in Russia. 'What's in all that space, Dad?' I asked, perplexed. He laughed, the eyes twinkling: 'Forest! Bears!' I was astonished and entranced: this was clearly something I had to see for myself. And where the vast spaces ended, the fascinating names began: Vladivostok, Magnitogorsk, Chelyabinsk, Krasnoyarsk, Baikal. I loved the sounds the names of the cities made, instantly wanted to speak a language which sounded like this. Because of the globe, and the atlas that soon followed, I won a housepoint at school for being the only seven-year-old in the short history of Gleadless Valley Housing Estate who could spell Czechoslovakia. I decided not to mention Novosibirsk.

From being very small, gap-toothed, two ribbons on top of my dark brown head, Russia became my secret world. The land where bears caught fish in torrents of white water, where the snow maiden walked in enchanted forests, where pencil-thin girls of impossible beauty pretended to be swans while the music played out its strange, heart-rending melodies. The music, from the first record of Swan Lake my Dad had bought me, played on in my head as I arabesqued clumsily in my gabardine mac around the petrol-rainbowed puddles through the estate, home to Landseer Drive, clutching my housepoints and my gold stars. As a child in primary school I knew nothing of the politics of it all and would have cared even less. It was the little swans of Tchaikovsky's ballet who danced endlessly through my head; it was the golden-domed churches and the mysterious forest that were calling me. And it was Dad that started it all - but it was another country first, and a different melody.

10

'People are the same everywhere...'

They were melodies in waltz-time mostly, the sort of haunting tunes that make you catch your throat in mid-phrase. These were the ones my father loved when I was small, the first music I ever heard, crackling out of the old radiogramme from the rigid, heavy seventy-eight rpm records. Dad always used to sing along with so many of these songs, he could never just listen. The names of the songs, the singers, the shows still echo around my head to this day: White Horse Inn, The Land of Smiles, Richard Tauber, 'Goodbye' by Josef Locke, 'Vienna, city of my dreams', music from 'The Merry Widow' and, above all, Dad's favourite, the wonderfully politically incorrect, 'Girls were made to love and kiss'. I can still hear the way his voice came in, always mid-way through a line, in his fine, high tenor. The words were always in English, but he never seemed to know all of them. For Dad and me, the melodies were always in the air, the words on the tips of our tongues. But they were not Russian at all. A decade on from those days in Caister Camp, and there it all still was in our Gleadless Valley living room: the language course, the library books and, above all, the music. The country that came first was not my secret land of bears and ballet dancers. It was Germany.

Dad had a book called 'Das schöne Deutschland' which he'd brought back from night school. It had fascinating gothic lettering on the front. I particularly liked the strange double dots the Germans seemed to like putting on the tops of their letters. 'Umlaut', a fun word to practise and roll around on my tongue: 'Ummm Lauaut'. The dots did things, Dad explained. Here was a bird, der Vogel. And now, here was a flock of birds, die Vögel

- and the 'o' had magically turned into an 'er' sound. Even more interestingly, there was more than one way of saying 'the', to show you if it was just one 'the' or lots of 'the's - and even to tell you whether it was a masculine 'the', a feminine 'the', or a neuter 'the' (neuter? and why did you need to know that anyway?!).

This was obviously something which preoccupied the Germans. This way, just by looking at the 'the', they could tell that 'the man' was masculine and 'the woman' was feminine, 'the boy' was masculine and 'the girl' was - neuter. Really?! 'Well, that's because the word for girl in German ends in '-chen', which is always a 'das' word, always neuter,' Dad said. 'Oh, I see,' I said, trying to look as if this was all perfectly understandable. The Germans, clearly, also had a lot of trouble with their spelling. 'W', of course, was pronounced 'V', whilst 'V' was pronounced 'F', except that they'd already got an 'F', also pronounced 'F'. This meant that a VW car was actually called a FauVay in Germany, which somehow sounded much less masculine to me, even though it was in fact masculine because the 'W' stood for Wagen, which was a 'der' word, which was masculine, which proved it. Dad explained all this as if it was really all quite obvious.

Sometimes we would practise the latest lesson on our walks down Lightwood Lane on a Sunday morning. Somewhere past the 'Derbyshire' sign the German would start. Dad would point at the sky: 'Wieviel Vögel fliegen in der Luft?' - 'how many birds are flying in the sky' he would say, and I would answer, 'drei' or 'sieben', depending on how fast I could count. German numbers were much easier than I expected - they'd had the sense at least to do those the same way we did. And then Dad would start to unravel the sentence, telling me things he'd learned at night school. 'Wieviel' sounds like 'Veefeel' because of the 'W' and the 'V', which you know, but it's also because when you have 'ie' or 'ei' it's the second letter which tells you how to say it. And there's more than one bird so it's not 'fliegt', it's 'fliegen', which is the plural.'

'But why is it 'in <u>der</u> Luft'?'

'Well, that's because it tells you where they are and so the 'the' changes again. It's called the dative case.'

'So what does the dative do?'

'Well ...'

It was somewhere around here that Dad got worried. A week or two later he announced that he'd decided to stop teaching me German because he thought it might be a bad thing. It might interfere with my school work and I should be concentrating on that. I was thoroughly disappointed. Though there were still bits of German I could do without authorisation. I could practise my numbers hopscotching down the paving flags on our street. I could have a go at the songs which sporadically appeared, with music, on the pages of 'Das schöne Deutschland'. When Elvis Presley was Number One with his version of 'Wooden Heart', my Dad miraculously turned up the German original. I could amaze my pals with a half-learned, half-made-up German version, 'Muss i den, muss i den ...', which was a big success until a classmate with a German mother turned up with the real words. Already it was clear to me that speaking foreign languages was what I wanted to do when I grew up.

I could also continue my secret lessons by sitting quietly alongside my Dad, deliberately not joining in so that he wouldn't stop me, as he followed a language course on TV. Dad had bought the record with the pictures of its stars on the front: Dieter, looking dark and intelligent, thoughtful and sensitive, and Anna (was it Anna? I like to think so) all petite and blonde, neat like a secretary. 'Komm' Mit,' it said, 'Wir sprechen deutsch'. And so they did speak German, every week on TV, halting at crucial moments to explain what they'd just said. The best bit came in the last programme before Christmas. After weeks of meaningful looks across the subtitles and the grammar tips, Dieter gave Anna her Christmas present and made her blush furiously and turn away. And the outlandish remark which had occasioned this shocked response? It was the way he had said 'you'; he had called her 'Du' instead of 'Sie'. It made him sound as if he were her boyfriend, or was trying to be, Anna explained to the bewildered English viewers. I was amazed at this obsession with the smallest words in the language. Not content with 101 ways of saying 'the', they could upset people with the wrong kind of 'you'. It was obviously a minefield, this business of venturing abroad, if a word like 'the' could tell you where things were and what gender, and 'you' could trigger love affairs with the wrong people. I couldn't wait to go and try it out.

My Dad, on the other hand, didn't seem to have any immediate plans to use his German at all. He simply went on from year to year methodically filling notebook after notebook with answers to grammar exercises and little bits of writing about Germany, holidays, my home town. The quiet progress from 'Das schöne Deutschland' book one to book two brought with it a growing renown as the only person in Firth Brown who could communicate with increasing numbers of German lorry drivers and engineers. Firth Brown's special steels provided the precision-crafted rolls through which much of Germany's steel production poured. But, at the very beginning of the 1960s, Germans were still a rarity in Sheffield, and the ones who came brought little English with them. My Dad was invariably drafted in to help – 'Run and get Frank!' - and quickly made friends of them all.

One I remember well was brought home to our house when I was about eight. Dad rescued him from the desolate stuffiness of one of Sheffield's best hotels for an evening by the fire in our neat little council house. They spoke German. Mum made tea. I sat and listened and was called on periodically to do my party pieces, of which the biggest success was my shaky German rendering of 'Silent Night'. It was nowhere near Christmas but, by the time I got to 'halt den Knabe mit lockigen Haar' there were tears in the kindly eyes of the far-from-home engineer.

Dad explained it to me later. It wasn't just some cute little kid unexpectedly singing carols in a foreign language, he said. It was the acceptance. It was the embracing of the former enemy. At a time when war films still poured out of Hollywood and the words 'nasty' and 'Nazi' were interchangeable for any comic-book villain, it could not have felt very comfortable to be German in an English city half-flattened by air raids, where a major city-centre site was still a tangle of charred and rusted girders. Even if Manchester City's Bert Trautmann had managed to become a hero of English football, words like 'Schweinhund ' and 'Dummkopf' could still be heard on any street where British kids played soldiers.

'People are the same everywhere,' Dad explained, teaching me the lessons he had learned in Caister Camp. 'There are good, kind people in every country. I've always thought the Germans are like us in lots of ways. The humour's not so different. You can relax with them. But it doesn't matter which country you're talking about: you have to look at the person first, not the country they come from, or what colour they are.' This was all going to come in handy later, when learning languages would take me on foreign adventures of my own.

11

'Knowing how to behave...'

Dignity was always a big deal in our house. It began and ended with my Dad who determined where the lines were drawn. When I was little I always wondered why I was the only toddler who was not allowed to scream and shout and interrupt the grown-ups' talk. I had to join in properly and politely, or sit quietly with my toys or my crayons in the parts which were obviously not meant for children. If this was frustrating in the beginning I soon discovered that it brought unexpected benefits. Years of 'knowing how to behave' taught me to look engrossed in what I was doing when I was really sitting and listening. If you don't interrupt with questions, I rapidly realised, people carry on talking and it's amazing what you can find out.

There was always a sense in our whole family that you never got anything if you didn't work for it. So Dad worked hard, rising through the ranks by his own smartness and conscientiousness, from being an apprentice turner at fourteen, to being a skilled machinist, a rate-fixer and, eventually, into management. Mum, however, 'didn't work' - in part, as she would say, because being drafted into the steelworks during the war had put her off for the rest of her life - but mostly because she was part of that post-war generation of women for whom not being employed outside the home was a mark of dignity. On our neat and tidy street most women didn't go out to work because they 'didn't need to work'. This put them, and, more importantly, their husbands, on a higher rung altogether than the women - of whom there were one or two round about - who 'had to go out to work'. This would sometimes be referred to in a hushed and disparaging way by the women who were more 'respectable'. 'Having to go out to work' suggested a workshy or irresponsible husband, too much beer and cigarettes, or too many children. All of which smacked of a lack of control and was self-evidently not respectable. Mum, and her other friends on the street, kept the house beautifully clean, did decorating, made clothes, shopped and cooked and visited elderly relatives, budgeted carefully, invited brothers and sisters round to tea and, on Wednesdays, went to the Gleadless Valley 'Young Wives' Club' which was hugely popular.

Being respectable and 'not needing to work' meant, in practice, never having much money to spare, buying the cheapest rather than the best, having modest pleasures and simple holidays. But none of this mattered when, by comparison with the desperate pre-war years, we had so much. A secure job for Dad, a whole house to rent just for ourselves, a garden to play in with roses and an almond tree, were all novelties to cherish. At the same time, all the post-war benefits of free health care and education beyond primary school offered a massive and previously-unknown sense of security. This, overwhelmingly, is what I recall of my childhood: the warmth of our house, the joyful dinnertimes when Mum welcomed me home from school and laughed and talked with me until I went back for the afternoon, the delight when Dad came home, the sight of my parents laughing and the playful hugging in the kitchen that made me feel so safe - in short, the feeling of absolute and certain love that filled our house. For years it was something I thought everybody shared. I never realised then how incredibly lucky I was to have a family like this.

So 'behaving properly' was a very small price to pay, even if, occasionally, it loomed larger than everything else. When I was about eight we went to Paignton on the 'English Riviera', as the railway adverts of the time described Devon and Cornwall. After years of Bridlington, Cleethorpes and Skegness, I experienced for the first time the miracle of warm sea. It was astonishing to run into the water and not start shrieking at the icy cold. But this was not the only attraction of the Devon seaside. Down by the magically red-gold sands there was a photographer's booth with a large, stuffed, skewbald horse permanently parked outside. I longed to have my picture taken on the horse to show my friends at home. Assuming that the photographer would niftily cut off the green wooden board to which the horse was glued in mid-clop, I imagined explaining that this was how I had spent my holiday, sitting bareback astride this monster animal, the effortless union of girl and horse, just like in our favourite television programmes, 'Champion, the Wonder Horse' or 'My Friend Flicka'. On the small, white-bordered, black and white snaps which adorned the booth, you could see that the moth-eaten bits of his ears weren't very obvious.

We were staying in a very nice boarding house in a street with a giant monkey-puzzle tree. The couple who ran it had a daughter just my age so I was allowed to play out in the garden. There were great big luscious breakfasts and fan-shaped Pompadour wafers in the ice cream and fruit salad for tea. It was the breakfasts that caused all the trouble. The fried bread, cunningly hidden under bacon and mushrooms, was extra-crispy. Two or three mornings into the holiday I cut into mine a bit too enthusiastically and watched both it and my fried egg fly off the plate and land on the carpet several feet away. The lady who ran the boarding house appeared promptly with cloths and brushes, mopping up the gooey yellow mess and smiling reassuringly at me. 'It's all right, don't worry. It's all right.' But Dad was mortified. He didn't think it was all right, and he certainly didn't think it was funny as I choked back my instant giggles. This was not 'behaving properly', it was doing the worst thing you could do if you were part of what they called 'the respectable working class'; it was 'drawing attention to ourselves'. My sweet and loving Daddy could barely bring himself to speak to me. I felt ashamed. But, later, down by the sands, I didn't feel quite chastened enough to prevent myself looking longingly at the stuffed horse. Unwisely, I asked if I could have my photo taken. Dad stomped off with the bag and the towels, muttering 'no' between clenched teeth. I trailed behind miserably with my bucket and spade, trying not to make any clanking noises which might remind him of my clumsy existence. I was obviously never going to get to the 'Horse of the Year Show' as long as I lived.

It never lasted long. In no time at all I had my longed-for photo and an ecstasy-inducing trip to the local riding school as well, as a holiday surprise. But Dad hardly ever had to say anything to me to let me know where the line was drawn. I hated to see the smile fade and to lose, however fleetingly, the big hugs and the pretend wrestling, the made-up games and the laughter. Even if being 'Daddy's girl', with a man like my Dad, created a confusion all of its own.

12

'A boy would have loved all this...'

I was the firstborn in the family and rapidly sealed my own fate as an only child. As my mother used to explain, 'after two years of you not sleeping, always being ill and screaming your head off, even your Dad had decided that one was enough!' But he was a man who loved children and, as my mother was always the first to admit, had been the one who would cradle me hour after hour, gently walking up and down the room in largely fruitless attempts to settle me down to sleep. And he would have loved a son, someone with whom he could have shared his passion for sport and the man's talk he enjoyed. Instead of which he was stuck with me, one of those children who always gets picked last no matter what the game, all the way through school. Despite which, there are endless photographs of me and Dad in which we are posing with bats and balls, me in shorts, attempting to look sporty. None of which helped in the 1950s, when girls were meant to be girly and know about girly things.

The houses on Gleadless Valley were a funny design. Ours was part of three sets of terraces, built round a rectangle, the back doors leading on to gardens which met up in the middle. On the side which looked out onto the street there was a brightly-coloured front door which led straight into the hall and the living room (for proper visitors) and right next to it, behind a door-high brick wall, was another door, drab-painted, which led into the storeroom and coal store and on to the kitchen. This was the 'back door', even though it was technically at the front, usually unlocked, habitually used by family, neighbours and tradesmen. The 'back doors' of the estate were a children's world, sheltered from the drizzle, cut off from the wind which howled across from the wilds of Derbyshire, special places of games and secrets.

The porch walls were the best bit. You could play two-ball without getting told off for making banging noises against the house: 'On the table, Betty Grable, in the hall, Henry Hall', 'Matthew, Mark, Luke and John, next door neighbour CARRY ON!' we would chant, yelling as the balls kept spinning from hand to hand. You could do handstands against the walls, practising delicate manoevres, like spelling OXO with your legs: hours and hours could be spent happily upside down. All of this was fine for a girl who spent most of her life in shorts and trousers, but it got much trickier when we were playing beauty salons and hairdressers, not least because the manicure set which every self-respecting 1950s girl possessed was completely unusable on me. It was Dad's fault I hadn't got any nails to manicure. Shortly after I acquired teeth, I had noticed him distractedly biting at his thumb and thought there must be something in it. It wasn't easy at first, but I was determined to discover the secret. Soon I had nails as thoroughly nibbled as his, which was when he had decided to explain that this was not a good idea for a young lady. It somehow didn't seem to be possible to point out that he should have said this in the first place.

It didn't take long before I realised that there were as many problems as pleasures in playing with the other girls. It was probably my own fault. I was younger than most of them, but it didn't stop me being bossy and a know-all. And I had some funny ideas which didn't go down too well. The worst one was when we were playing house, which we did all the time. Once I'd made the astounding discovery that there were other places that were different, where people didn't speak English, I would insist on making this my contribution to the game. 'I'll be a foreigner,' I'd say. (Much later, with unsuspecting school friends, I would give full rein to my little Slavic obsessions: 'I'll be Czechoslovakian,' I'd say, to puzzled looks all round.) When I'd pulled this off a couple of times my small friends would all groan, knowing they were in for an afternoon of heavy mid-European accents and spells of interpreting between me and an imaginary official speaking gobbledygook: 'Ee sez eet eez no gud, you cannot com een.' Eventually, a stop was put to this by the concerted actions of the others: 'We're going to play house, but you can't be a foreigner!'

They didn't seem to realise that this took all the fun out of things. If I couldn't be a foreigner, I couldn't really see the point of the game. Not having any brothers or sisters, I never knew how to do the stupid arguments properly. Problems with the girls were a big factor in my tendency to play with boys. It was just a lot less complicated. Me and the other boys would rush outside to play cowboys and Indians. Or sometimes we'd play at deep sea divers, a game I'd invented based on an underwater nature programme we all watched. We would pretend to be wearing flippers and oxygen masks, like our TV heroes, Hans and Lotte Hass. We'd move up and down the road, bent forward intently, moving our arms and legs in slow, exaggerated circles, breathing noisily. The shiny bits of gravel on the road all went into our 'pearl' collection, which formed the central object of the exercise. Better still, this particular choice of TV heroes allowed me to carry on doing my foreigner routine perfectly legitimately, picking up bits of twig and shouting things like, 'Luk, Hens, a rasor shell!' Sometimes we would hurl ourselves onto the floor, dramatically grappling with octopus, or choke violently as our oxygen ran out and we would have to be resuscitated back on the boat on the pavement. It was a lot more exciting than sitting about in beauty salons.

But the sad fact of the matter was that I entirely lacked the skills to become an acceptable son-substitute. Dad was always the natural sportsman, someone who could play any sport he turned his hand to. He was a naturally talented footballer who, after making a habit of dislocating his shoulder in awkward tackles, still couldn't bear to give it up and so became a referee. He was a cricket all-rounder who was a valued member of the Firth Brown team. From the word 'go', his sporting prowess was a total mystery to me. I recall one occasion at Roe Lane, Firth Brown's sports ground, when he seemed to be interminably in the centre of the field instead of coming to play with me. When he finally came in, raising his bat to acknowledge the spectators' acclaim of a brilliant cricketing century, the significance of it escaped me completely. I just felt put out that he hadn't managed to be caught out earlier. For his part, my Dad was, I am sure, appalled to realise that he had produced a daughter who had virtually no hand-eye coordination at all. There I would stand in my shorts and plimsolls looking, as I thought, sporty and businesslike, an image I could maintain as long as I never got near a ball. Many a time I would run up to a stationary football and resolutely kick, only to see it remain where it was or wander a miserable few feet away.

Worse still, I couldn't really see the point of team sports in the first place. When I was seven, I won a very nice autograph book for coming second in the egg and spoon race at Prestatyn Holiday Camp, one of my few athletic successes. Not knowing any celebrities at the time, I asked my Mum and Dad to contribute the first signatures. My Dad carefully provided a nugget of wisdom which he thought I would find useful: 'Never be afraid of taking part because you might not win. Remember, there are many more losers than winners.' And he was right; they were words I often thought of as the years went by. But I sometimes wondered if he had really written them for himself. Certainly, the advice could seem a bit rich, coming from someone as relentlessly competitive as he was.

As I got older Dad would sometimes take me off to the local matches he was refereeing on a Saturday, a process which involved lots of fascinating preliminaries. There was the packing of the sports bag which we chanted through together: 'me shoes, me socks, me shorts, me shirt, me collar and cuffs and me plastic bag.' There was the all-important testing of the whistle and the singing of its song: 'Oh, oh, oh, oh, what a referee, what a referee, what a referee! Oh, oh, oh he's gone and lost his pea and his little wooden whistle wouldn't whistle!' There was the prolonged reading of the Daily Mirror in the toilet ('what's Dad doing?' 'He's reading') which I only recognised years later as an antidote to stage fright. Finally, there was the tortuous bus journey down through the endless houses and flats of Gleadless Valley into the central bus station, across all the platforms and out again, miles and miles, on a bus to somewhere like Swallownest. I used to make up stories from the names on this particularly picturesque bus shelter sign - 'Swallownest, Catcliffe, Treeton'.

All of this was wonderful and ensured my Dad's undivided attention. But when we got to the match, off he would go into the dressing room, talking to players, chatting to the linesmen if there were any, and, however friendly everyone was, there was no getting round the fact that for ninety minutes (an hour and a half!!) I was stuck with watching twenty-two men kicking a ball around. I would try so hard to look fascinated for at least twenty minutes but, in the end, he would always catch sight of me dreamily swinging on railings or looking for four-leafed clovers. Even grass seemed more riveting than forty-four bare legs in muddy boots. Sometimes Dad would try to liven things up by giving me the 'Sheffield and Hallamshire' league fixture list to peruse, but even this ploy failed miserably. I remember the day he realised it was useless. He was watching my delight at realising they wouldn't go into extra time and seeing stupefying boredom written on a face where polite interest usually tried to rest. He told me that he wouldn't bring me again, that there wasn't any point and he looked, bewildered suddenly, at his programmes and his sports kit and said, almost to himself, 'a boy would have loved all this'.

I went on trying for years to be a boy. I climbed trees down Lightwood Lane. I didn't mind being cold and wet. I jumped over streams and raced over stiles. I wore trousers and shorts a lot. I continually took painful lumps out of my knees and didn't cry. I made friends with other boys. I played with toy cars. And the girls, sniffing out a peculiar hybrid, like a pack of dogs spotting a barking cat, never quite trusted me and often excluded me from their games. It was a painful and perplexing business, this attempted boyhood. But, in the end, I found the secret, the path to shared pleasures with Dad that would last me a lifetime. I could talk and I was learning to argue. So if I couldn't be a sporty boy it didn't matter. I would have to try and be a brainy one instead.

13

'Get thee glass eyes...'

Just because I no longer went to the matches it didn't mean, of course, that the football disappeared. We simply adopted a different approach which worked rather better. Saturdays in our house, for decades, were dominated by 'the match'. Long after my Dad had given up trying to turn me into a footballer it was still vital to be interested and attempt to become knowledgeable about the all-important game. As he ironically observed, someone who spent Monday to Friday as a rate-fixer would obviously be 'uncomfortable not being abused' on a Saturday. The answer, clearly, was to pursue a career as a referee. In all, he spent 13 years on the Football League line, so there was never any shortage of football-related research material in our house.

Top of the list there was the Football Association Handbook for lesson one: learn all the teams in the Football League.

'Test me on these, Dad.'

'Why are Norwich called the canaries?'

'Because they wear yellow and green.'

'Who wears claret and amber?'

'Bradford City.'

'There's a funny thing about Bradford City's ground, you know. They haven't got room for a changing room for the officials inside the ground. You have to get changed in a terraced house across the street and come up into the ground through a tunnel!'

And off he would go, peppering the quiz with reminiscences. He liked Halifax Town because they produced a witty programme with Shakespearean quotations for all the roles in football (Referee: 'Get thee glass eyes', King Lear, Act four, Scene six) but his favourite was Rochdale - 'they've got nowt, but you can have half'. Mansfield was the fixture he dreaded, not because there was anything wrong with it, just that it was impossible to get to on public transport from Sheffield. Endless journeys on circuitous routes to end up virtually a stone's throw from home drove him mad. Though he would often get back in any case incredibly late after night matches, waiting for connections on deserted stations in Lancashire, riding back to Sheffield on the milk train. Most weeks there were little local treats from the venues he had been visiting: Doncaster butterscotch wrapped in silver paper, Pontefract cakes with their luscious bittersweet flavour, boxes of kippers from Grimsby for my Mum to cook for a Saturday night tea.

We used to go on tour with him when the venues were interesting. He would head off for the match, clutching his sports bag, and Mum and I would be let loose on the city. My Mum liked Liverpool and Hull the best, where we could wander down to the docks and look at the big boats with the names of exotic home ports painted on their sterns. If my Dad provided the interest in languages, it was my Mum who supplied the hankering for foreign shores. I preferred Manchester because, once out of the rain-sodden centre, we would make for the delights of Belle Vue zoo. My other favourite was Grimsby because it always gave us a day in Cleethorpes to mess about on the sands and the fairground rides. At the end of the day, we would go down to the end of the prom opposite the station and watch my Dad, lithe and athletic after the match, leaping across the gravel-covered bollards in the sands from the station platform. Though it always felt sad leaving Cleethorpes; you could hear the roundabouts forlornly playing 'Anchors Aweigh' as the train pulled out, leaving the sea behind again until the next time.

There was always plenty to do with the football, even if going to the match wasn't part of it. Every Saturday night we would sit, eating cheese and biscuits, watching 'Match of the Day'. Then there were programmes to collect and pictures to cut out of the paper.

My Dad kept a scrapbook and we would look through The Green 'Un every Saturday night for reports of his matches. Sometimes there were even pictures of him, black shirt and shorts, green arms and legs, sending somebody off at Killamarsh, signalling a penalty at Swallownest. Once he got onto the Football League line the pictures sometimes turned up in the national newspapers, properly black and white, next to the famous names of the day.

I was always disappointed that he couldn't referee a Sheffield match because it was against the rules; we were avowed Sheffield Wednesday supporters in our family. In the end even this was rectified when he was asked to officiate at an evening testimonial match for Wednesday's Redfern Froggatt. To my delight, my Dad came back with pages of my autograph book covered in the signatures of all the Wednesday stars: Tony Kay, Peter Swan, David 'Bronco' Lane. He was appalled when, soon after, they were banned for life and sent to prison in the corruption scandal which rocked football in the 1960s. 'What a waste,' he kept saying, 'when you've got all that talent, all that future in front of you.' And he would tut and shake his head, looking disgusted, 'It's greed, Susan, that's all it is. Look where it gets you.' For my part, the criminal convictions certainly added a bit of spice to an autograph book otherwise lacking in celebrity. It didn't occur to me that, for five minutes at least, my Dad would soon be the biggest football celebrity I knew.

14

'A mark of appreciation and goodwill...'

Until the mid-sixties my Dad worked as a rate-fixer in the Light Machine Shop at Firth Brown. It was an exhausting and thankless task, one which he was happy to forget about once he got home and very rarely talked about. He would walk into the house, regular as clockwork, his suit smelling of steel dust, and, just as regularly, pull his trouser pocket inside out to reveal his finger stuck through a sizeable hole. The ritual was always the same. My Dad, expression like a naughty schoolboy, would say, 'sew me a little hole in my trouser pocket, Joyce,' and my Mum, standing over the cooker, would respond, 'again?! You do it on purpose just to annoy me!' and his grin would grow wider, watching her pretend annoyance.

So his world of work was one of which I knew little except on the one special occasion each year at shutdown when I would get to see something for myself. When the works closed for two weeks in summer, the furnaces ceased firing and the men left on the annual holiday, Dad would go down on the first Saturday morning to sort out his rate-fixing paperwork. He would take me with him, to my great delight, into the office with its high windows fronting onto Saville Street, to play with the typewriter. We would stand and look at the huge and silent machine shop where the giant steel cranes kept watch and then Dad would steer me to what seemed an enormous desk, an adjustable typing stool and a massive old Imperial with keys that hammered blue and red ink onto the paper. I would sit for hours, whilst he worked on his calculations, engaged in what I thought were important jobs like typing out the words to the hymns I'd learned at Gleadless Valley Methodist Church's Sunday School:

'Consider the lilies of the field how they grow,

They toil not, neither do they spin, (stop typing blue, change to red)

Yet Solomon in all his glory,

Was not arrayed like one of these' (change back to blue, new paragraph).

At dinner time we would walk up to Petre Street where I would run into the house, proudly waving my technicolour hymn sheets, 'Look what I've been doing, Grandma! We sing all these at Sunday School!' 'Oh, that looks nice and neat, love,' she'd say, wiping her hands on her pinny before she'd touch the treasured papers. And, for me, this production of 'proper' writing to treasure for the next year was much more vital than whatever it was that had taken Dad down there after everybody else had left. This little annual ritual at shutdown made it the only week when I didn't take flowers for my Grandma. It was another thing my Dad had a decided view about: 'Lots of people take flowers to graves every week but the person who's died can't see them. I often think there are people who show they care more when someone's dead than they ever did when they were alive. Take Grandma some flowers now while she can enjoy them and know that you care about her. It's better than putting flowers on graves when it's too late.' So I'd take flowers down to Petre Street every week and watch whilst Grandma poured a handful of salt and dropped an old penny into the water to make them last. As I got older I had the idea of buying colour-coordinated blooms for silver and golden and ruby weddings, all of which saw me religiously putting into practice Dad's philosophy on flowers for the living.

If shutdown allowed me a glimpse into Firth Brown's machine shops, it was far more important to me that it gave me some time to spend with my Dad. And, in any case, Firth Brown was forever turning up at home, however far away we now lived from Pitsmoor's grimy streets. My first drawing books were discarded blueprints, neatly guillotined into stapled rectangles, with the white side covered in childish scrawls and the blue reverse with its pale outlines of steel machining jobs meticulously marked to the nearest thou. When the rubber wheels of my third pair of roller skates turned square from use my Dad took them to work and replaced them with steel: I had the noisiest, shiniest skates and the best-developed calf muscles on Gleadless Valley. Later, when I developed an interest in rocks and minerals he would come home with bags of turnings, all to be carefully explained then neatly labelled and recorded in the 'rocks and minerals' exercise book. These spiralling pieces of Firth Brown's special steels gleamed in solid, jagged-edged metallic blue, concertina-ed in springy necklaces of grey-brown, glowed in golden-purple stiffened ribbons. They looked beautiful set out on the table against the sunlight with their resounding, majestic names blocked out on card: carbon chromium, chromium vanadium, chromium molybdenum, chrome moly-vanadium, nimonic – this mixture of nickel and chrome the hardest, shiniest example of them all.

My Dad was just thirty-nine when he completed twenty-five years service with Firth Brown. In other firms, such as Brown Bayley, it was a regular practice for any worker to receive a mark of gratitude which had some value, most frequently a gold watch or clock. Outside of Sheffield steel other companies in the scientific field in particular might well be handing out significant cash sums at special presentation dinners for their most loyal workers at this period. Not Firth Brown. My Dad came home with nothing more than a certificate. 'Look at this!' he said, laughing and handing it round. And he told the story of how one of the directors had turned up in the office to present it to him and had had some difficulty believing who it was for. My Dad never remotely looked his age, except in the worst throes of illness, and, at thirty-nine, was still the fresh-faced young lad who appeared to have no business receiving a Long Service Certificate.

It was a beautiful thing, though, and I was fascinated by the pictures around its scrolled edging of roses, daffodils and thistles. There were Victorian sepia portraits of Thomas Firth and John Brown in the centre, the Sheffield coat of arms at the bottom and, at the top, the Firth Brown Atlas Works emblem depicting Atlas holding the globe on his shoulders. ('Do you know who that is?' Dad had asked when I was doing a project on mythology at primary school. 'Isn't it Atlas?' I'd replied, pleased at showing off my knowledge. 'No, it's me,' he said, 'that's just what I feel like at work!') In the corners of the certificate were beautifully-coloured miniatures of steel production: casting, rolling, forging and machining. Like so much else at Firth Brown it had been produced in-house, as one of my Dad's friends later recalled, 'It was designed and printed by a man called Frank Mortimer, and he was the head postman. We had a whole postroom in those days, it was quite a flourishing little affair. Frank Mortimer was in charge, he was a little fella, bow-legged, only just over five feet. He fought in the First World War, in the machine gun company. And he did that certificate and he got twenty-five pounds for doing it. Mind you, I suppose it was a lot of money in those days, but it took him months and months of careful work to do it. It's marvellous really, for a man who wasn't trained.'

At the age of ten, I was taking the entire business completely seriously and expected to see the certificate duly attached to the wall. I was still admiring it when my Dad said, 'Right, that's enough of that,' and slung it up into the loft where it remained for the next twenty years until he discovered elaborate and intricate textile industry certificates from Bradford junk shops decorating my bathroom wall. 'If you're going to stick stuff like that up, you'd better have this one,' he said, evidently feeling that the wall beside the toilet was an appropriate place for it to end. It took me some time to realise why the Directors' 'mark of appreciation and goodwill', as the certificate's inscription put it, had had such a reception once outside the bounds of the works. Part of the answer was supplied immediately in discussions I heard of common practice elsewhere. But the bigger picture was one I only pieced together much later.

The way Firth Brown's loyal staff were rewarded was something I heard comments about over the years. Usually, they turned up in conversations which I overheard rather than took part in, though the picture they painted was confirmed to me later in the reminiscences of my Dad's friends. Firth Brown was an incredibly successful firm; so successful, in fact, in the particular, highly-specialised products they made that customers used to have to wait for the steel they'd ordered. There was simply nowhere else to go. The result for the directors at the height of this boom was a lifestyle of fabulous and apparently bottomless wealth. Their habit of lavish entertaining was well known to their employees, as was their practice of using the firm's chauffeurs to hang around until two or three in the morning for them outside a night club, or to run them at the drop of a hat to an airport.

Against this backdrop the managers and staff were always underpaid, simply because they were their own people who'd come up through the ranks. When the firm had no need to look beyond its walls for managerial recruits it could also avoid paying the going rate. In later years, on the occasions when the firm had to go out to the market to recruit, it was not unusual to find that the new appointees were getting £2-3000 a year more than people who'd been in Firth Brown for thirty years. Even by the 1980s, this could be almost a third more on an annual salary for those at or near the top of the ladder. It was a practice which created inevitable and huge ill-feeling.

Even in the early sixties, as I watched the long-service certificate fly into the loft, there was such an obvious mixture of loyalty, pride and annoyance at the firm's unwarranted penny-pinching in my Dad's attitude to his place of work. 'It was a benevolent autocracy,' was how he would describe the firm years later. But this curious mixture of emotions about Firth Brown was something I ran into again and again over the years and it was still there in the memories, long after the firm had disappeared. As one of my Dad's manager friends put it when my Dad was no longer around: 'It was a sad day really to see the thing decline the way it did. It was a tremendous company really, Sue. But they didn't look after us.'

15

'Come on, lads, we're marching on London...!'

My Dad chose to say very little of all this in front of Mum and me at the time. But there was endless discussion of other things which interested him, football being only one of them. My Dad was always a natural fixer. It was getting things done, 'getting things to my liking', as he always put it, that interested him. He liked to be involved in things he could do something about directly, so party politics in the 1950s didn't come into it. Not that he didn't have an opinion. We were in the midst of what our next Labour Prime Minister, Harold Wilson, was to call 'thirteen years of Tory misrule', and there seemed to be little prospect of change. But Dad left us in no doubt as to what he thought of the Conservative government, little of it flattering. And, finally, his annoyance galvanised him into joining the Labour Party.

My Dad was a big fan of the new Labour leader, Hugh Gaitskell, and was happy to support him in his attempts to get rid of the Tories. But what finally sent him off enthusiastically leafletting and canvassing was the imposition of a new, unelected Prime Minister in 1963. Sir Alec Douglas-Home was not even an elected Member of Parliament, he was a hereditary peer, brought in from the House of Lords. My Dad was utterly disgusted and outraged that something so undemocratic could happen in the 1960s: 'it's feudal, they think we're still living in the Middle Ages. They think they've got the right to rule.'

If Douglas-Home was the spur to action, Aneurin Bevan had been the inspiration. Bevan was the minister in the post-war Labour government who became the architect of the National Health Service. He had a sonorous Welsh voice and a remarkable turn of phrase. My Dad and his friends went to see him at a memorable rally in Sheffield City Hall: 'He was a most wonderful orator, Susan. He could make you believe anything. If he'd said, "come on lads, we're marching on London!", we'd all have got up and gone'. Neither Bevan nor Gaitskell were to live to see the Labour government my Dad was canvassing for. He was dumbfounded at Gaitskell's sudden death and ardently followed the ensuing leadership contest, hoping George Brown would be defeated. 'Why don't you want him, Dad?' 'Because he's a buffoon'. He was pleased at Harold Wilson's election and loved his dry wit and deadpan delivery.

My Dad, I'm quite sure, was never a radical, nor even particularly left-wing. He was far too much of a beneficiary of the fifties when we'd all 'never had it so good,' as our then Prime Minister, Harold Macmillan, informed us. In our family's case, of course, he was perfectly correct. Although my Dad's own politics by the 1960s were, in reality, only slightly left of centre, he enjoyed playing around, sounding more radical than he was when it suited him. On one famous occasion he'd been sent on a management course with Ken Bliss and they had been put up at the 'Olde Blue Bell Inn' at Barnby Moor in Lincolnshire, only to find that some gathering of local Tory dignitaries was going on at the same time. As they all assembled in the bar with much self-congratulatory back-slapping around Quentin Hogg (one of my father's most detested politicians - the subsequent Lord Hailsham), Dad and his friend broke into a rousing chorus of the 'Red Flag'. Back home, he told us this tale with great hilarity. My Mum was horrified at his daring in the face of someone she had only ever seen looking important on TV. Not that Hogg himself was likely to have been disconcerted, though the sound of an impending Labour victory was by then getting harder to ignore.

Though my Dad was never a radical in party political terms he was still prone to radical ideas which he would try out on anyone who would listen. The best example was his transport policy which involved a major shake-up of the local taxation system, the 'rates'. 'What they ought to do,' he would say with unfailing regularity, 'is put bus fares on the rates. Everybody would pay for them directly when they got their rates bill and, after that, everything would be free. So everybody, pensioners, large families, everybody, would be able to travel as much as they wanted. And, because they'd be used so much, there'd be plenty of buses, properly paid for, so there'd be good services wherever you lived. That way people wouldn't need to get their cars out. So there'd be much less traffic, so the buses would get there quicker. The city would be cleaner, there wouldn't be any traffic jams and everyone would benefit.' 'But what about people with cars,' I can remember asking, 'wouldn't they be fed up about paying for something they didn't use?' 'But the rates are like that already. The biggest item on the rates is education. Not everybody has children but nobody suggests we shouldn't all be contributing to children's education. You can't have people just paying for what they use because it's selfish and, in the end, it's not economic. I think the council ought to take me up on this!'

Oddly enough, 'the council' did do something very similar some twenty years later in the short-lived cheap fares policy of what was popularly known as the 'Socialist Republic of South Yorkshire'. Though, by this time, my Dad had moved on to other things and the politicians he detested the most, apart, inevitably, from Margaret Thatcher, were now in the Labour Party. But back in the sixties, Dad and my primary-school self were firmly on the same side. His transport policy was one I always enjoyed trying out on any friend who seemed to have an interest in buses. It always went down well. We knew hardly anyone who had a car. But it was a different business once I had been propelled by the Eleven-Plus examination through the mysterious, well-polished portals of the 'High School'.

Sheffield High School for Girls was a 'direct grant' school, part fee-paying and part-scholarship. It was a member of the Girls' Public Day School Trust (motto: 'Knowledge is now no more a fountain sealed') and was the natural home of the daughters of the heavily-outnumbered Sheffield bourgeoisie. On their home turf, arrayed in heavy brown tweed coats and ludicrous felt bowler hats, they fought a handsome rearguard action against any incursion from the city's gigantic council estate sprawl. In my very first term at the school, in 1964, the country finally elected its long-awaited Labour government under Harold Wilson with a programme which included the abolition of the Eleven-Plus and the introduction of comprehensive education. The school's immediate response was to claim to be more egalitarian than anything a Labour government could achieve. As it became clear that it would in the end be obliged either to join the masses in the state system or become totally private, a special assembly was held to reassure us that any change would be beyond our own school lifetimes. This was an immense relief to me after listening to discussions at home about whether they had any chance of paying school fees when I had already been forced to witness my parents' looks of horror at the price of the school uniform.

Our headmistress delivered her speech from the stage, swaying from foot to foot in her long black academic gown and squinting at us from above her spectacles. 'When people ask you about the ethos of this school, about what it stands for,' she intoned, 'you should tell them that, of course, we have always been the original comprehensive form of schooling, because we have always taken the brightest and the best girls of their year, regardless of their social background. And in that sense' - and here she thumped the lectern - 'you should tell them that <u>we</u> are the true comprehensive school.' As a good and conscientious new pupil I carefully explained all this to my Dad when I got home. To my surprise, I was met with a loud and cynical guffaw in response. It was lucky, I thought, that he hadn't been present at the assembly. Life at the High School was quite complicated enough without my Dad bursting into the 'Red Flag'.

16

'Oh, I dig elocution...!'

I had never heard of Sheffield High School until the 11-plus application forms came round. Parents had to write down the grammar schools they wanted their child to go to in order of preference, in case they passed the examination. The school you were allocated depended on the results you got. In those days, boys were expected to do a lot better than girls in the Eleven-Plus. This was because, as everyone knew, boys were better at exams than girls. They were less emotional and more intelligent. And, anyway, girls didn't really need a grammar school education because they would only go and get married and have children and stay at home. There was no need for them to have a job, much less a profession. What no-one ever told you was that there were actually more grammar school places for boys than for girls, which meant that the boys' pass mark was a lot lower. In my primary school class before the exam girls and boys were very evenly split in the test results they scored each week. But when the Eleven-Plus results came out only three girls had passed for grammar school. Eighteen boys received grammar school places, many of whom had regularly scored less well in the tests than the girls who now found themselves dispatched to the local secondary modern school as 'Eleven-Plus failures'.

I had just assumed I would put High Storrs and City Grammar at the top of my application form like everybody else would. We all knew about the top grammar school for boys: everybody had heard of King Ted's and knew that only the cleverest boys ever put it at the top of their list. But this girls' place was a complete mystery.

'Is it Catholic like that other one?' I can remember asking when the subject came up at home, vaguely thinking of Notre Dame grammar school. 'I don't think so,' my Mum had said, 'I think it's the ones you sometimes see in town on Friday afternoons with the funny hats and the big coats.' 'Oh, I thought that was a private school.' I was having some trouble understanding the concept of the 'direct grant'. 'Look, it says here that they only take up to twenty-five girls a year through the Eleven-Plus and that you've got to make it your first choice, so we should put it down first and have done with it,' my Dad said, decisively. 'But that means we lose a choice!' I protested, not thinking for a minute that I might qualify. 'You're not going to need all six before you get in somewhere,' he said, clinching the matter. I didn't like taking the form back into school, I knew nobody else would have put that place on their list. I had to blame it on my Dad.

My parents were absolutely thrilled when the results came out. My Dad was so proud he couldn't stop grinning. 'You're a gudgeon, Susan,' he said, in one of his favourite manglings of the English language. I felt pleased that they were so pleased, but not so sure about venturing off into the unknown. Everything about it seemed designed to single you out. It wasn't just that it was the only school in the city that didn't have a regulation gabardine mac, or the awful bowler with its luminous yellow ribbon, or the sheer expense of it all. It was things like the Friday afternoons off or even the dates of the terms. When everyone I bumped into from my year at primary school was already excitedly describing their new schools and showing off their uniforms I was still kicking my heels around the block in my primary school frocks and cardigans. 'Haven't you started yet?!' my former classmates asked, incredulously. And then there had been the open evening for the newcomers and their parents.

We had walked into the vestibule with hushed voices. It was a very far cry from the brick and glass of Hemsworth Primary. The polished wood seemed to go up and up, covered in the gilded names of long-past Oxbridge entrants with incomprehensible words like 'exhibition' written against them. There were pictures along the corridor of the aristocratic founders: Lady Maria Grey, Lady Mary Gurney, Lady Emily Shireff, Lady Stanley of Alderney (funny name for a woman, Stanley, I thought). Whilst our parents got the pep talk in the school hall, we were marched off on our tour of the premises. Everyone around me seemed to have been in the adjoining private junior school or a similar establishment elsewhere. 'Of course, I've recently started having elocution lessons,' one of them was saying. 'Oh, you've only just started? I dig elocution!' came the improbable response. We didn't talk like that on Gleadless Valley. By the end of the evening I was beginning to think it would be better if I didn't talk at all.

Still, it did have one very obvious redeeming feature: it had a real art studio. Up at the top of the winding wooden stairs, its huge row of windows slanting against the sky, was a room of wonders. There were, to my eleven-year-old eyes, rows of fabulous paintings and astonishing life drawings on the walls, there were proper easels and pots and pots of paints, there were cases of books full of art treasures I'd never seen before. I didn't want to leave. I could imagine sitting for hours in this room, listening to the rain on the skylight windows, watching the light changing as it fell onto sheets of art paper. I could almost taste that wonderful silent concentration, the total absorption that a careful drawing demands. If Firth Brown had stopped my Dad from getting anywhere near his paintings I was doing my best by now to take up the brushes on his behalf. I knew that this was going to be my place in this school, even if the rest of it felt as alien as Saturn. I was beginning to look forward to my first day.

It wasn't an auspicious start. There were plenty of very obvious drawbacks to this new school: the chafing of the stiff collar, the rubbing of the slightly large new shoes, the weight of the coat and, worst of all, the extra-terrestrial headgear. On my fifteen minute walk to the Gleadless Valley bus stop above Rolleston Woods I could almost feel the curtains twitching at the extraordinary spectacle of a small council estate kid in a would-be public school uniform. It was torture passing anyone in the narrow gennels, seeing the expression of unfeigned amazement on their faces, feeling like someone who had turned up at a fancy dress party on the wrong day. But all of this was nothing compared with what was to come. It was the disaster of the medical certificate.

We had all been sent a sheet of paper to fill in with dates of all our vaccinations and childhood diseases. I was quite proud of mine. Always one for catching every infectious disease in the book, I had also managed to make time for bits of exotica of my own, like scarlet fever and a particularly violent and prolonged episode described at the time as 'nettle rash', not to mention the sudden high drama of acute appendicitis. It looked good, I thought, all written out in neat blue ink with the dates my Mum had spent ages trying to remember: it was a wonder I had ever got to school at all. The letter from the High School about our first day said we should just bring it along with us to hand in. What it did not say was that 'medical certificate' at Sheffield High School had the same force as 'password' at Colditz.

As the girls of all ages poured through the doors the certificates were rapidly gathered in. I felt around desperately in my stiff new satchel, knowing without even looking that the certificate was still sitting on the sideboard at home. There was nothing for it but to melt into the crowd. 'Halt!' commanded the gatehouse guard in the forbidding shape of the school secretary. Trained to sniff out imposters in High School uniforms, she had me spotted in an instant. Mauling my expensive new coat she pushed me to one side on the steps where I stood on my own, in abject fear, waiting to feel the rifle butt in my ribs if I so much as twitched. When everyone else had gone in she rounded on me and a couple of other, much older, miscreants, demanding to know where our certificates were, handing out our punishment duties. She wasn't remotely interested in hearing that this was my first day. For people who forgot their certificates there could be no entry into the inner sanctum: we simply had to go back home and fetch them.

I don't suppose it had ever occurred to anyone introducing this regime that not everybody at the High School lived in the leafy south-west suburbs. As I was to realise very rapidly, living on council estates was just not something that High School girls did. It took me all morning to trek out to Gleadless Valley and back. My mother was in the middle of the washing, her face looking up from the ringer a picture of horrified astonishment as I walked back in. I was all set to walk straight back out again in my anxiety at what this school appeared to be like but she made me sit down and have a warm drink, recover my composure a little before setting off again at a less hectic pace. Both my parents were angry at what had happened to wreck my first day. 'What would she have done if I'd gone out?' I could hear Mum saying as soon as my Dad got in. No doubt, if we had lived in the city's bourgeois belt, the school would have been treated to the irate parental phone call. As it was, they both blamed themselves for sending me off ill-equipped. And, anyway, we didn't have a phone.

The repercussions of this unfortunate morning went on for the next seven years. By the time I got back to school, heels well blistered from hurrying in the bright new shoes, it was almost the dinner break. My form mistress, a young and kind, newly-qualified teacher, looked at me in appalled disbelief when I explained the reason for my absence. 'I'm sure it could have waited until tomorrow,' she said, helpfully. 'Still, you're here now, Elizabeth, so that's all that matters.' Some time during these first miserable hours my absent self had been recorded in the register under the wrong name. Every single year after that I would have the same conversation with a new form teacher:

'Susan, you're down here as Elizabeth.'

'That's not my name, it's a mistake.'

'Oh, is it your middle name?'

'No. It's not my name at all.'

'Oh, I see. When did you change it?'

'I never changed it. I've never been called Elizabeth. I've never told anyone I was called Elizabeth. It's not my name.'

'Well, it says here you're Elizabeth.'

They never got my name right on their forms through my entire school career. It somehow seemed to sum up how out of place I always felt. Though I could never admit it at home. It would have been unthinkable to tell my Mum and Dad, so proud that I was at a 'top school', that being clever still didn't make you good enough.

17

'We suggest a minimum donation of five pounds...'

The jolt to the system of that ridiculous first day never seemed to diminish during the whole of my first year. I was totally unprepared for what I encountered beyond the doors of the High School. Everyone seemed to be the daughter of a lawyer or accountant or doctor. They all seemed to think the steel industry was some peculiar pastime that poor people went in for somewhere in the mucky bits of town. They made extraordinary statements you were supposed to agree with: 'I think everyone has a second bathroom downstairs nowadays, don't you?' 'I don't think anyone just has holidays in England any more, do you?' and, worst of all for someone who had been brought up on a diet of horse-racing, the killer sentence, 'I think most people in the class will be getting a pony this year, don't you?'

The school didn't help. Not content with selecting a uniform you couldn't buy at anywhere reasonably priced, they had compulsory 'extras' like tennis lessons in the summer with a professional coach. I can still see my Dad's expression on reading the letter about the additional fee for this one. He knew he would be paying it for social reasons only. All our years of attempting ball games had proved to him conclusively that even British tennis champion, Christine Truman, wouldn't get me to hit a tennis ball the other side of the net. I felt mortified just handing him the letter.

And then there was the interesting question of the school library. In my first year the school decided that the library needed an extension and a committee of parents was set up to oversee the fund-raising. The High School had no intention of turning itself into a venue for bring and buy stalls or anything as common as tombola; extortion was more the house style. I was already cringing before my Dad even opened the official letter composed by a leading local solicitor-parent. 'We suggest a minimum donation of five pounds,' it said. My Dad was outraged. Five pounds was a great deal of money in the mid-sixties. In fact, it was just under half of my Granddad's best ever weekly wage. But I was sent back to school with the large blue note carefully sealed in an envelope. He didn't want me to look different from the other girls.

Only I couldn't help being different, even in an identical uniform, trying to do all the right things; after all, you couldn't buy a new accent with the Cole Brothers' credit account which had paid for the pricey uniform. It didn't come home to me immediately what kind of a world I had walked into, but a couple of weeks into term something happened to bring the picture into focus. We were all sitting waiting for a teacher to arrive and a conversation was going round the class about the best way to get somewhere or other. It was all very inconsequential until I joined in and made some remark about the bus. It was the full Sheffield 'u' that did it: suddenly the room was full of peals of laughter and everyone was trying to copy my quaint pronunciation. I tried to pretend it was funny, but it wasn't, and it didn't get any more amusing as time went on; there were clearly more languages than French to be acquired in this particular building.

By Christmas I was learning to be more careful and beginning to make some friends. It was party season and there seemed to be a competition for the most remarkable event. I was invited for the first time in my life into suburbs like Dore and Totley, into rambling Victorian houses with immaculate furnishings, or taken with a whole group of classmates to the Sheffield Playhouse to see the Christmas show. The entertaining was on a scale I had never encountered before. It was astonishing to see the luxury my new friends took for granted, the possessions they had, the excessively complicated arrays of knives and forks they could manoeuvre, the staggering size of their Christmas trees. And I realised, quite quickly, that I was often arousing equivalent interest. Partly it was because I had always been good at quizzes, mostly it was because of the Sheffield accent. I could feel their parents watching me, evidently wondering how this urchin had got into their house. When it became apparent that I was not going to filch the silver or set fire to the dog they would begin, metaphorically, to pat me on the head. 'Oh, she knows all these answers!' or 'Oh, isn't she quick!' they would marvel at some nifty move in a game I was playing. Sometimes it amazed me to find that, back outside the house at the end of the day, I was still in Sheffield. I wasn't used to feeling like a refugee in my own home town.

As long as it was just me encountering this kind of thing I didn't mind too much. In any event, I was so outnumbered there didn't seem to be any way around it. Although it really bothered me that I couldn't imagine inviting any of them back to my house. They probably thought they would need passports to get onto Gleadless Valley. I was thirteen, I am ashamed to say, before I overcame my embarrassment about this, and only then because my parents' careful calculations and saving had led to the purchase of a neat pre-war semi in Millhouses. Their pride in the house and the telling details which surrounded its purchase made it clear to me that their discomfiture had been not dissimilar to mine. I remember my mother saying that she'd found the paper shop and would put in an order to get the Daily Mirror delivered as usual. 'I thought,' my Dad said, looking up from his tea, 'we might take the Daily Express instead now.' There was no discussion as to why this might be; everyone tacitly understood. But my Dad was fantastically proud of his house, loved the garden with its mature trees and shrubs. He was so pleased that I thought he'd be sure to buy a name-plate for it as other people on the street had done. 'What do you think we should call it?' I asked, expecting a serious discussion. 'Millstone,' he said, smiling wryly. It took me a while to realise he was referring to the size of the mortgage.

18

'If you haven't already got a pony, when are you going to get one...?'

It was only when my Mum and Dad were obliged to confront the realities of having a daughter at the 'High School' that all of these issues of social class came to matter to me a great deal. I didn't like all the business around the tennis and the library but it was the ponies that really caused the trouble. Before we left Gleadless, two of the girls in my class who had ponies decided to set up a 'Pony Club' for everyone to join. We had to fill in a questionnaire to get our badge. Most of it tested our knowledge of horses so it was no problem to me at all but, at the end, it got a bit more personal. 'If you haven't already got a pony, when are you going to get one?' it said. The answer was obviously never but I put a non-committal 'don't know'. I was appalled to see that the only other girl in the class who lived anywhere near my side of town had written 'in the summer'. This was awful! I was going to be the only person left out of the Pony Club! When I was probably the only one in the class who, thanks to Granddad, could list all the Grand National winners since the end of the war! In my anxiety about all this, I started going on about riding at home. I just couldn't stop myself.

The trip out to Dore Moor horse show was supposed to be a treat. Dad took me up there, bought me a programme and tactfully kept at a distance after I'd met up with my classmates and their ponies. It wasn't a very happy afternoon. I always seemed to catch up with them just as they trotted off for another bit of the showground. There was clearly no chance of getting even a whisper of a ride. The day began to drag, despite my resolute attempts to appear engrossed. By the time we set off for home my Dad was looking thoroughly morose. 'I hated watching her trailing around after those girls with the ponies,' I heard him telling my mother later. He started doing some serious sums. All through that summer I felt that turbulent mixture of desperate childish longing and the beginnings of grown-up common sense. Most of all I felt ashamed that all the wanting had let my Dad see how unbridgeable the gap was between us and them, how even someone with 'a good job' in the steelworks was no match for a born and bred professional, and the money they had doubtless inherited, when it came to providing ponies and all the paraphernalia that went with them. And if, at first, I couldn't stop the longing, later I began to hate my other world of school, and all the things it stood for, for doing that to someone who worked so hard, who was so skilled, who deserved better.

It wasn't all bad, of course. There were other aspects of the school which I appreciated deeply. There were entirely new subjects which engrossed me, there was a library full of books and there were teachers who, for the most part, had a deep love of their subjects and a great talent for conveying their fascination. Above all, there was the art studio which never failed to live up to its early promise. But, on a social plane, there was no disguising the fact that, in the mid-sixties at least, the school was dominated by snobbery and an utter blindness about the world in which most people in the city lived. Still, it was nothing if not an education. And it did have its moments of light relief. In the course of my first traumatic year at the 'original comprehensive school' there was a school debate on transport policy, no less. It raged on for some time with lots of interventions from the floor until I managed to bring proceedings to a standstill with my Dad's radical proposals for the buses and the rates.

Suddenly the room was full of people protesting on behalf of the poor car owners who were about to be robbed blind to subsidise feckless bus-users. I realised with a jolt that I had never been in a roomful of car owners before. I tried the education argument; it was surprisingly unsuccessful in a school where over half those attending were paying fees already. It was clear that Dad's transport policy could only be viewed as curious and quaint. Acting as his ambassador I felt even more than I usually did in that environment that an ocean the size of the Atlantic separated even our proudly-purchased semi from the huge Victorian piles the girls in my class inhabited. But Dad, at any rate, was delighted that I had had the courage to speak up in such surroundings and concluded with the satisfied observation that car ownership was not sustainable and that history would prove us right. Which made me feel a little less of a freak than before.

At home, of course, I never felt like that. As I settled into my teens, Dad and I would talk and argue around the politics of the day and watch the protagonists on the news and programmes like 'Panorama'. We would spend hours trying to put the world to rights until, when we realised we could go no further, my Dad would round things off with one of his favourite phrases: 'Well, it's like I always say, Susan - the higher, the fewer!', and we would burst out laughing at this deliberately nonsensical conclusion. It was important to my Dad that I was well-informed and had an opinion on everything; he wasn't concerned at all if it wasn't the same as his. And, if these opinions sometimes put me at odds with other girls in my class, this was no more than I had become used to over the years.

As an uncertain teenager locked into a school for the gentry in which I felt hopelessly out of my depth socially, the talking was a mixed blessing. Within the halls of the school I could use it as a weapon against those who looked askance at what remained of my Sheffield accent. Later, through the anxieties of Christmas dances at other, co-ed, schools or the tongue-tied miseries of the local youth club, the talking and arguing, whenever I finally did manage to open my mouth, was immediately identified as unwelcome by boys looking for a comfortable evening's snogging. I was left in no doubt that 'normal girls' weren't like this; that, if they had anything very much to say, the clever ones pretended they hadn't. We really hadn't come very far from the 1950s. London might be the centre of a global youth revolution by the mid-1960s but girls were still supposed to be decorative and were not expected to have opinions.

It was only after I arrived at university that I came to appreciate that, if I had the High School to thank for the qualifications which took me there, it was my Dad, who had left school at 14 with none, who had shown me what the point of education was. That there was no sense in knowledge unless you could use it to look, to consider, to challenge, and that then you would be prepared, you would be armed, for an encounter with other people's worlds.

19

'You had your own napkin...'

The Christmas Eve revels apart, rate-fixing at Firth Brown must have been the perfect testing-ground for would-be management. No doubt it had occurred to the powers-that-be in the firm that anyone who could flourish in that environment had probably learned all there was to know about getting your own way. Certainly it was the rate-fixing which gave rise to one of my Dad's favourite phrases. Whenever he thought I was trying to pull a fast one he'd say, 'give over, Susan, you're kidding to a man who's kidded to thousands!'

Firth Brown was a firm which, in those days, sought its talent in-house, training up smart lads for jobs in management. By the mid-sixties, Ken Bliss and my Dad found themselves setting off on parallel paths into the management of the Light and Heavy Machine Shops. My Dad had been working as a rate fixer for thirteen years by this time and no doubt assumed that he would do the job indefinitely. Certainly, it had never occurred to him to think of himself as management material. So he was not expecting to be offered the post of Senior Foreman in the Light Machine Shops, particularly as it came with the proposal that, in due course, he would take over from the present manager who was approaching retirement. I well remember the mixture of surprise and pleasure in his voice and his proud expression as he described what they were suggesting.

Moving into management back in the 1960s brought a far greater change to a way of life than it would do today. The jolt of moving to a monthly salary, paid in arrears, took a bit of thinking about. There would probably be a cash advance which would have to be paid back, there would be no more overtime to earn. On a practical level it meant opening a bank account, a serious business in those days when credit was hard to come by and banks were choosy about their customers: 'For one of the guarantors, the company will agree to stand. You will be required to find a second one,' the appointment letter said. Still, my Dad didn't think about it for long. At the very least, the shift in power relations was going to make a pleasant change from rate-fixing. As he later recalled, 'Senior Foreman was a job with a lot of authority and which suffered no abuse from anyone. There was only one problem, other than those of a technical nature, and that was that thirteen or fourteen others were convinced they should have had the job before me. But this was a problem which disappeared fairly quickly when, after a year, I was appointed Manager of the Light Machine Shops which at this time employed over 300 men and twenty-two shop stewards.'

Finding himself as a member of management in a firm such as Firth Brown was a source of considerable pride and a certain degree of amazement. He was fascinated and, I think, quite tickled to discover that there were one or two highly-civilised perks of the job, most notably the near-ceremonial reception into the Managers' dining room. As one of his manager friends described the process to me much later it all began with the receipt of a formal invitation: 'it said, "If you will present yourself at the Mess on such and such a day, the President will meet you and conduct you to your chair." You had your own napkin, you had your own place.' Yet, oddly enough, my Dad's management of the Light Machine Shops turned out to be of relatively short duration. Just as the Senior Foreman job had come as a surprise, a new offer was soon to come his way. He was certainly not looking for a move; it was simply that a job needed doing and he seemed to be the likely candidate. Out of the blue, they asked him to become Works Manager of Firth Derihon.

As the neighbouring Sheffield steelworks of Thomas Firth Ltd and John Brown Ltd had expanded and developed, a group of companies had emerged. In the 1920s, their collaboration had led to the establishment of the Brown Firth research laboratories. Their subsequent amalgamation in 1930 produced the firm of Firth Brown. Building on the two companies' previous acquisitions, the holding company of Thomas Firth and John Brown developed as its major concerns not only Firth Brown, Sheffield, but also Firth Brown, Scunthorpe, as well as Firth Vickers, in part ownership. Firth Derihon played a key part in this group of companies and was based on two sites at Tinsley in Sheffield and at Darley Dale in the heart of the Derbyshire Peak District.

Ever since the war steel production had been a political football. The nationalisation of the steel industry was a major pledge of the 1945 Labour government, a policy immediately overturned when the Conservatives returned to power in 1951. Now, in the mid-1960s, it was once more a hot political issue. The nationalisation of the steel industry, for the second time in twenty years, was one of the principal economic policies of the Labour government led by Harold Wilson from 1964. Yet, this time, the mechanics of the nationalisation process were to be rather different.

In the first, post-war, nationalisation virtually all steel manufacturers had been included. In the mid-sixties the decision was taken to base re-nationalisation on tonnage, including only the largest bulk steel producers. At a stroke this eliminated many companies producing special steels for the aerospace and nuclear industries from the nationalisation process. The tonnage of steel they produced was not considered to be great enough for inclusion in a new state-owned steel giant, despite the fact that the value of their output was massively greater than that of companies such as ESC which were included. Firth Brown was the biggest company left outside the state umbrella with a tonnage which fell just short of the required level. The ramifications of this were to be felt throughout the years to come and, most fatefully, under a government with a very different ideological stance.

20

'King of Darley Dale...'

Left outside the state umbrella Firth Brown had to fend for itself and efficiency was of the essence. Firth Derihon had a problem – and it was my Dad who was drafted in to fix it. He had been taken out to the Darley Dale Die Shop to see whether he would be able and willing to apply his knowledge to the issues which were troubling them: a need to move the work through the shop more efficiently and 'slack' rate-fixing. On the basis of his visit my Dad produced a report which he described as merely 'a tentative conclusion' after such a nodding acquaintance with the plant. Yet, in it, he suggested a reorganisation of staff to help address the two key problems they faced and pinpointed inefficiencies in machining. Watching an operator struggling with a Die, he observed that, 'the operator could barely see the position in which he was cutting and was spending almost all his time in fitting a gauge.' He had made a drawing of what he had seen in order to stress the point: 'the Die would have been more easily machinable if, instead of being on a Lathe, it had been on a Vertical Boring machine as the rough sketches show. Do you have a Profiling attachment for a Vertical Borer? If not, this would prove invaluable.'

But it was the experience gained through years of rate-fixing which, as his bosses had correctly spotted, would prove crucial and was central to these first observations: 'I thought that the Piece work system was very unsatisfactory. The principal functions of any payment by results system should be that it gives the company the results it requires and at the same time is easily understood by the people to whom it is applied. The system at Darley Dale appears to fall short of both these requirements. I consider a rethinking of the whole system could well be beneficial.' At the same time his recommendations for staffing underlined the conviction he always maintained that hands-on knowledge of processes, rather than theoretical training, was the key to efficiency. Proposing an internal appointment of an additional rate fixer he commented that, 'I feel that such a person would bring to the job a knowledge which would not be readily available to a new person, even one trained in Work Study methods.' The bosses at Firth Brown were clearly impressed with his conclusions and promptly offered him the job of Works Manager, coordinating production at the split sites of Tinsley and Darley Dale. There was only small snag: how was he going to get there?

My Dad was already in his forties and had never sat in the driving seat of a car. But with twenty-five miles between the firm's two factories, gaining a driving licence in the shortest possible time was a prerequisite for accepting the job. He bought a second-hand VW Beetle and simultaneously arranged his first lesson. It was the rush hour and the driving school was situated on one of the main routes out of Sheffield city centre. Off he went, in his first moments behind a wheel, straight out into the stream of traffic, on and off the clutch up the hill, negotiating the buses and the lanes for the traffic lights until, several miles later, he finally turned into a quiet road. His instructor put his test application in the following day. A couple of months later, after much driving around in the Beetle with qualified relatives and friends, he passed his test in a similarly dramatic fashion after the test car handbrake came off in his hand on the first hill. The examiner immediately offered him another test date but he insisted on continuing his prolonged series of handbrake-free hill starts around the inclines of Nether Edge. It was a shame the RAF had never spotted his fighter-ace talents.

After years of trailing down on two buses to the grimness of the east end, you could hear him singing in the bathroom in the mornings at the prospect of a sunlit run in his car over open moorland and down through the Chatsworth estate. Even more pleasant was the discovery that he now had a small empire to call his own. 'I should have stopped there,' he used to say, years later, 'I could have been King of Darley Dale by now!' He would come home full of fascination at the things he could do, the wildlife he'd seen en route and unexpected aspects of working out of the city. One of these was what he described as the very different nature of the Derbyshire workforce, the more relaxed and less abrasive attitudes on the shop floor, which had both its positive and negative sides.

He loved to recall one of the few occasions when he had seen the people at Darley Dale get upset. The company had decided to send in a team of work study experts to speed up processes on the shop floor. One of their recommendations involved the handling of drop forgings. They had been watching the men using huge pincers, arms held wide, to lift and transport the steel across from one position to another. If, instead of holding the pincers horizontally, they crossed their arms and flipped the steel over, the work-study team concluded, the operation could be effected far more rapidly. There was only one snag with this idea: the steel was red hot. 'Can you imagine it?' my Dad would say, grinning broadly. 'They got us all together to explain. Oh dear! I thought we were going to have a riot! They'd never have got out of the factory if they'd tried that in Sheffield!'

As time went on things at Derihon got better still. They won an order to produce parts for the huge aero engines Rolls Royce were making for the USA's RB211 jet. It was a prestigious project to be involved in and ensured that Derihon and its people were thoroughly scrutinised by visiting American specialists whom my Dad always described as 'very tough'. But he loved it. He loved showing off his skill and that of those around him, was always intensely proud of what Sheffield special steels could do. At least as much he loved the unexpected pampering that went with it all: the visits to Rolls Royce at Long Eaton, the little tours of the beauties of the Peak for the visiting Americans, the expense-account lunches in traditional country inns and hotels to oil the wheels. Dad would take us out in his car at weekends and say, 'We'll just call in here,' driving into places like the beautifully oak-panelled 'Peacock' at Rowsley so that we could listen to his stories of entertaining the Americans in suitably evocative surroundings. They were good years, the Derihon years. Looking back, I can't ever remember feeling anxious about him once. Something that could certainly not be said of the years that followed.

21

'Foul and abusive remarks to a linesman...'

Just as the Derihon years often seemed a high point in my Dad's life in steel the late sixties were a great time for the football too. My Dad never made it onto the Football League 'middle', much to his annoyance. At home, in private, he would complain about what he was convinced was an unchallengeable culture of nepotism within the Yorkshire League at the time. Nevertheless, by the mid-sixties, he was becoming a regular figure on the line at big matches. Mum and I were becoming used to his regular appearances on 'Match of the Day'. Annoyingly, he often seemed to be running the line on the same side as the cameras. We would get glimpses of him as they took corners, the unmistakable bow legs bouncing into shot for two seconds at a time. On what was to become the most celebrated occasion in his career, however, the match was not televised but it could scarcely have attracted more publicity.

It was a home match at Manchester City and my Dad was on the line immediately in front of the City bench. If their manager, Joe Mercer, was the benign face of this increasingly successful club it was their volatile coach, Malcolm Allison, who grabbed most of the headlines. Flamboyant and outspoken, with a taste for the high life, Allison was one of a new breed of football celebrities. He had made himself a part of London's rock-star culture, frequenting the most fashionable nightclubs, being photographed on nights out with glamorous people, wearing his trademark fedora hat. But, as far as my Dad was concerned, this was just another match, just another fixture he was covering for the love of the game, certainly not for the minimal expenses linesmen received in those days.

As the game unfolded and decisions went against City, Allison repeatedly jumped off the bench and treated my Dad to his colourfully-expressed point of view in front of the packed stands. It must have been one of the few times he was glad of the experience of non-stop aggravation that Firth Brown's rate fixers' office had provided him with. Certainly, he was not about to be intimidated by a football coach, however 'industrial' the language. Carefully doing his job, he jotted down the comments, complete with expletives, in his notebook and warned Allison that he would be reported to the Football Association if it happened again. My Dad was never one for making idle threats. To Malcolm Allison he must have looked like just another amateur official he could easily bully. So he just carried on. By the following day, much to the amazement of my Mum and me, there were Daily Mirror reporters in our house wanting to know if it was 'true that you're considering legal proceedings against Mr Allison', a suggestion that both amused and astonished my Dad.

The Mirror published a wonderful picture of the hearing that followed. In an ante-room outside the chamber in Leicester where the FA Disciplinary Committee was in session the wide-angle lens captured Allison and Mercer leaning against the wall whilst, twelve feet away, propping up the opposite wall, my Dad stood, arms grimly folded, awaiting the verdict. In due course Malcolm Allison was found guilty of making 'foul and abusive remarks' to a linesman and fined £100, a considerable sum in 1968. The linesman in question was rather more delighted at the lifetime ban from the touchline which the Committee also handed Allison, a decision which seems astoundingly draconian when compared with the way football's celebrities are treated today. We all watched the BBC news together with great delight and satisfaction that night. Though it must be admitted that my Dad was less than pleased with another of the pictures printed in some of the national dailies the following morning. As they had left the FA, still without speaking, Mercer had suddenly swung round on the steps outside and held out his hand to my Dad. Reacting automatically, he had shaken hands as the flash bulbs popped, niftily spun, to his instant disgust, into the 'happy reconciliation' shot for the benefit of the waiting press photographers.

Four years later my Dad was annoyed to discover that an appeal against Allison's lifetime touchline ban was in the offing. By this time Malcolm Allison was so much the playboy manager with the flashy lifestyle and eye for publicity that my Dad assumed the FA would simply crumble in the face of celebrity pressure. It was with some satisfaction that he read Malcolm Allison's comments in the paper the following day: 'I thought they'd be prepared to forgive and forget. I am bitterly disappointed that after all this time I cannot win a reprieve, but really there is nothing else that I can say or do.' My Dad, I think, felt both gratified and vindicated. Not that he had any axe to grind against Allison himself; rather that he believed rules should apply equally to everybody. He was pleased that being rich and powerful hadn't been enough to swing the decision. It appealed to his sense of fair play. It was a nice example of the expression he always enjoyed using: 'I'm just getting things to my liking, Susan,' he'd say.

22

'Keep out of the corners...'

I was in my mid-teens by the time my Dad was approaching the football officials' retirement age. As a linesman, forty-five was the limit of the top-flight career. We were still spending Saturday nights together, munching cheese and biscuits to the strains of Kenneth Wolstenholme's commentary ('Oh, dear, listen to him,' my Dad would groan, 'he doesn't half talk daft sometimes'), when the discussions of life after football began to get serious. My Mum and I were dreading it, we couldn't imagine what he would do with himself. Besides, we'd got used to missing him on a Saturday: if it wasn't the football, it was cricket in the closed season. By now, my Mum and I had our own well-worn Saturday entertainments which we had no wish to modify for a bored and - literally - sidelined referee. But, before the day dawned, in his very last year on the line, he finally got something he had always dreamed of - a European Cup match.

The venue could not have been more perfect for my Dad. It was Bayern Munich v. St.Etienne, not just championship football, but Germany too. My father flew off with the two other British officials for three unprecedented midweek days off work. There were tours of Munich and trips to beer cellars, meetings with legends like Franz Beckenbauer. But best of all, as far as my Dad was concerned, no-one had thought to provide an interpreter and scarcely anyone at the club could speak English. My Dad was overjoyed. As the crowning glory of all the years wrestling with German grammar it could scarcely be bettered. Everyone was delighted at this unanticipated stroke of luck in finding a German-speaking Englishman.

It was like Christmas when he got home. At a time when referees were paid peanuts the presents from the European clubs seemed astonishing. There were gorgeous and beautifully packaged French chocolates and a gigantic 'Diorissimo' eau de toilette from St. Etienne. There was a gold watch with the team crest, Munich beer mugs and an Adidas bag filled with sports gear from Bayern Munich, quite apart from the presents he'd bought for us himself. But his greatest delight was in the present which had cost them nothing: in recognition of his services to interpreting, Bayern Munich had presented him with the match ball on departure, signed by every member of the team. It was all a bit of unadulterated pleasure and, as a footballing swan song, made for the happiest possible memories. By the end of that season it was, as someone once said, all over.

In the event he didn't get under our feet much at all. He could still be a spectator, unexpectedly switching his allegiance to rugby league and turning into a supporter of Castleford. And there was always the fishing. From an occasional day out this was turning into a regular pastime under the tutelage of friends who knew what they were doing. His regular partner was Jack Howard, his old friend from the rate-fixing days, who was now running a pub in the east end of Sheffield. Jack was a well-known character in the locality who could always be relied upon to entertain my Dad. He loved to recall the time someone, in considerable annoyance, had accused Jack of being 'a fly bastard', to which Jack's laconic response had been, 'Well, I've been a prisoner of war, a rate-fixer and a publican, so if I'm not a fly bastard now, I never will be.' On the fishing trips, my Dad would provide the transport and Jack would provide the river. 'Do you think we'll catch anything at this place, Jack?' my Dad would say. 'Catch anything?! I tell you, there's two foot o' watter and three foot o' fish!' was invariably Jack's response.

It wouldn't have been easy to keep the footballing going even if he hadn't been forced to stop. By the end of the decade work had become dramatically more demanding. There was simply less space in which to cram everything he might like to do. Though he would still regularly bump into old refereeing friends in town or get asked for advice by young men in his Machine Shop who were just starting out with the notebook and whistle. He once showed me something he was writing for a newly-qualified referee who had asked for some tips. He had drawn a rectangle with goal posts and had shaded in a lozenge shape on top. 'This is what a football pitch looks like at the end of the season,' he had written, 'Motto: keep out of the corners.' Yet, by now, for my Dad, League football was a thing of the past. Always unsentimental to a fault he gave away his collection of programmes, threw out the old, worn boots. Even the Munich ball went eventually. The football remained on the television only and in conversations over a glass of beer. But it was good to remember, even in a small way, being part of the glory days. And, as the sixtes drew to a close, there seemed to be all sorts of stuff in Sheffield to be proud of.

23

'Do they think we all look like this...?!'

Sheffield!
Now there was a name to conjure with in the sixties.
Sheffield - Steel City!
Sheffield – City on the Move!
Sheffield - the third largest city (in area) in England!
Sheffield - the city (just like Rome!) built on seven hills!
Sheffield - the city of five rivers! (repeat after me: the Don, the Sheaf, the Rivelin, the Loxley, the Porter).

Sheffield - the city with the cleanest air in Europe! (the what?! - I thought this was Steel City!) Ah, yes, but the Clean Air Act had whisked away all those nasty smogs and now we were scrubbing and sand-blasting to reveal the shiny heart of Shiny Sheff. No longer Victorian England's 'dirty picture in a golden frame', the Sheffield Star and Telegraph's annual 'Golden Frame' calendar could now proudly feature full-colour photographs of the bright and blossoming City Centre.

And this was only the beginning of the superlatives. There was the Biggest Display of Christmas Lights Outside Oxford Street! which ran for miles, all the way from Castle Market, up through Fargate where the newest bits, like the prancing reindeer direct from last year in London, bounced in the wind above the bus stops, and on and on, all the way down The Moor, with a little pirouette in Barkers Pool outside the City Hall for good measure. What Oxford Street saw last year, we could have this. No wonder the buses brought in the Christmas shoppers from all over the north, including (imagine!) Blackpool, the home of illuminations, itself! The Council merrily spent a fortune putting us on the Christmas map until more stringent times were heralded by the arrival of a large stainless steel globe opposite the Town Hall. This was where grateful Sheffield citizens were supposed to deposit what bits of cash they had left after paying their rates bills to save up for next year's lights.

But it was worth coming to Sheffield for the shopping. After all, we had the Largest Number of Department Stores Outside London! It was true: quite apart from the predictable national chains like Woolworths and Marks and Spencer and British Home Stores we had a whole series of huge stores all of our own. There were Atkinsons and Robert Brothers on the Moor, there was Cole Brothers on the prime site in Barkers Pool, there were Walshs and Cockaynes down the bottom of Fargate, all locally owned by real people. When I was in the sixth form, delivering the Christmas post, I was delighted to learn that Mr Cockayne was on my round. He had huge picture windows which allowed me to glance nosily, if discreetly, at his leather armchairs and polished table tops. You might think we're a bunch of northern clods, I used to think, aiming this remark at nobody in particular, but there's no rubbish in this lot. You want to come and have a look, teach yourself a thing or two!

It wasn't difficult to amaze out-of-townies, if we ever met any, with all this kind of stuff. After all, we also had a Publicity Department in the Town Hall whose job it was to produce the official Sheffield Christmas Card and the successive glossy brochures which we could all learn off by heart. Back in my early teens I was dead impressed: the entire city's collective chip on the shoulder must have been floating about in my quota of the clinic orange juice.

Most of all, though, at the beginning and end of the city's burgeoning civic pride there was, of course, steel. Even if you had nothing to do with it (although most people seemed to, one way or another) it was inescapably at the heart of Sheffield's entire identity. Vulcan, the God of the Roman steelworks, as we liked to think, stood proudly atop the Town Hall as a symbol of the city.

Our steelworks dominated the landscape for five miles to the east of the city centre. Their production was worth billions; and it was classy stuff, everyone said, not like this 'clog iron' they turned out in Wales and Scotland. It was puzzling that we, as a city, didn't seem to be more appreciated. Even in my early teens, I could manage to feel part of the collective misunderstood.

Perhaps it wasn't difficult to see why. Every time the regional news decided to ask the opinion of the 'person in the street' in Sheffield you could guarantee that the first and last talking heads would be women in curlers with fags hanging out of their mouths. It was as if the TV crews piled out of the train from Leeds at Midland Station and just nipped up the hill behind to the colossal Park Hill flats. 'There's a typical Sheffielder!' they must have yelled, pursuing the women in turbans and pinnies up to the vertiginous walkways which had by now become the city's signature. 'Nice shot, Nigel!' the directors must have said (cut to mouth open, ash dropping, curlers tossing, city panorama background). I can still hear my Mum groaning now, 'Do they think we all look like this?! Can't they find anybody who's got dressed?!'

But, of course, they couldn't because they'd come from Leeds and this was clearly a covert attempt by our great Yorkshire rivals to undermine the jewel of the South Yorkshire economy. After all, what did boring, mercantile Leeds have anyway? Tailoring. Too many red-brick terraces. Only two department stores. Only one football team. A city centre of such economic insignificance that even the Nazis couldn't be bothered to bomb it. Whereas we had steel, which was crucial; we'd been obliterated in the war and risen like a phoenix from the ashes. We had steel, not iron, in our souls; we were self-evidently more heroic. Even the newly-built M1 had decided to stop at Sheffield for what would have been the point of it going any further? All we lacked were the television studios and this was obviously a temporary oversight. Long-term, me and my friends all thought, it was as clear as daylight which city was going to come out on top.

24

'Getting into the music...'

Ron and me were very into Sheffield's programme of urban regeneration. We used to walk into town on Friday nights to admire the development of the inner ring road and the sand-blasting programme. We did this because nobody would go out with us. Which was because boys never spoke to us. Which was because we never smiled at them or gave them any encouragement. Which was because we were really cool. And completely tongue-tied.

Ron had been my best friend since I was thirteen. I had always been a bit in awe of her – Veronica could somehow even manage to make the High School's awful brown bowler look funky. She always seemed to be about a fortnight ahead of me. We started going to school dances together. We never actually spoke to anybody but we did do lots of posing just in case anybody was ever going to be brave enough to wade past the ice-cool stares we'd perfected. And we were great dancers. I'd always been a bit of a 'twist' specialist myself back in primary school when it was the one and only dance to do. I had been very put out when the twist abruptly fell out of fashion and I had to start inventing my own steps. Veronica always seemed to know the steps to any brief dance craze that followed - she must have glued herself to the dance demonstrations by the earnest young people in sweaters on 'Ready, Steady, Go'. She was always way ahead with new shoes, especially, appearing in black patent and chunky heels before everybody else, or realising at once that the only things which could be worn with a very short skirt on a blistering summer day were obviously knee-high boots. She had wonderfully straight hair, the most crucial fashion accessory of the sixties, whilst I had been the only girl in primary school with curly plaits. I was still busy flattening as much of my head as possible when Ron walked in one day with a bubble cut. I had simply not noticed that even men were having perms by this stage.

As the sixties wore on and we were approaching 'O' levels we had discovered 'progressive' music. All of a sudden the last thing you were allowed to do was dance. Ron and I would sit in her bedroom on a Sunday afternoon with the algebra on the floor and John Peel on the transistor radio. I was hopeless at maths and Ron was brilliant at it; sharing the 'progressive rock' was the only way I could get her to do my homework for me. In the 'city on seven hills' an afternoon listening to Radio 1 was not as comfortable as it sounds. We lived in the shadow of Brincliffe Edge where the signals for the BBC's newest station had to fight their way through the trees on the escarpment. We didn't actually move much when we were listening. And we certainly didn't smile. We wore scarves and big earrings and sat for hours in public places 'getting into the music'. We sat, looking mournful, swaying slightly, through endless City Hall concerts whilst white guys with permed hair and flares sang the blues. And then there was the 'blues night'. Ron and me, you have to understand, knew Pete Stringfellow when his club was in a basement under a shoe shop. Well, we didn't actually know him, of course, but that didn't stop us telling everyone that we did.

Tuesday was 'blues and progressive' night underneath the shoe shop. We had to go every week. Well, we had to be seen there. Mostly we had to be seen by a particular group of lads who kept turning up at our youth club on a Sunday night. We were all incapable of speech. I don't know what their excuse was but ours was definitely the result of years in a single-sex school. Being in this environment for any length of time seemed to have one of two effects on all its female pupils: either they became crippled with shyness in the face of the aliens known as 'boys' or else they were renowned for running after anything in trousers. ('This seems a singularly unfortunate piece of casting,' one of our teachers had been heard to remark on realising that a leading member of the nymphomaniac tendency was playing the Virgin Mary in the Christmas nativity). As we were firmly in the former camp we could not be expected to speak to the boys we were interested in, even if they were sitting at the table next to us. We would all just sit there, clutching our cokes, nodding our heads to the deafening wail coming out of the speakers.

One week Ron and me were thrilled to discover that John Peel himself was actually going to be guest DJ for the blues night. It was packed. And there was John Peel, looking just like he did in the Radio Times, large as life behind his turntables in the corner. We were so excited by this we had to sit down and ignore him like we always did everybody else. After all, you wouldn't want to look uncool, would you? I mean, like you'd never seen the person most famous for developing 'progressive' music in Britain before, would you? Hardly anybody spoke to him all night. We were all locked into the same bit of barmy behaviour. As the evening wore on, the poor man evidently became increasingly mystified by his apparent ostracism in the corner. In the end he was practically pleading with us to go and ask him for a record. Ron and me thought about it. But we decided not to. What if we asked for the wrong sort of thing? He might think we were peculiar.

Sheffield at least offered us places to go when we were in our silent and miserable phase. We could watch the lights change colour on the Goodwin Fountain at the top of Fargate. We could walk behind the cathedral to Paradise Square and read the plaque commemorating 'John Wesley's largest crowd on a weekday'. We could wander up the Moor past the closed department stores and pick out dress fabrics in the windows. Or we could walk to our favourite spot of all: Furnival Square. There it was, newly built, two concrete semi-circles and a bridge over the inner ring road. You could run over the bridge, shout from one side to the other, sing and dance your way around this intriguing bit of architecture. And what was the really big attraction of this futuristic section of the 'city on the move'? There was absolutely nobody there.

It had to stop. We knew it really, if we were honest. One day we would have to rediscover the power of speech. But when a disorder is as incapacitating as this the remedy can sometimes be more painful than the condition itself. In the end, we realised, there was just nothing else for it: we would have to join the Young Conservatives.

25

'Dear me, my daughter in the Young Conservatives...'

Vicky's Dad was standing for the council. He was going to stand for the Conservatives in Walkley. ('In Walkley?!! - is he a masochist, or what?!') He was going to need some help leafletting. I was not surprised to hear this at all. I shouldn't have thought the Tories even had a local party organisation in Walkley. But, if they did, they didn't seem likely to be of an age to cope with Walkley's dizzy gradients on a brisk morning's leafletting. Even in a place like the High School I thought Vicky would be doing well to find any volunteers. I couldn't think what she was looking at me for. 'George is going to come and help. He's promised to get his friends along. We'll have a drink and something to eat afterwards. Do you think you could come and help?' Well, of course I could! No problem! See you on Saturday!

George was Vicky's boyfriend and he went to King Ted's. Vicky was one of the bold little group who regularly arranged trysts over the wall with their boyfriends from the huge, rambling King Edward VII school for boys across the road. The wall in question was at the very far end of the school grounds. It was strictly out of bounds. Talking to boys was absolutely not allowed under any circumstances whilst on school premises. This extended to circumstances other schools regarded as quite normal. The sixth form had once asked if they could hold a dance. 'Why, certainly,' our headmistress had responded, 'but there must be no stiletto heels and no boys!' They decided not to bother.

The question of the 'Melbourne Avenue wall', as it was known, excited constant concern. 'Girls have been seen, once again, hanging over the wall on Melbourne Avenue! This will be severely punished!' the headmistress would announce at assembly. It never seemed to stamp the problem out. But members of staff were assigned to patrol the grounds and shout at people and the matter was 'taken up' with the head of the boys' school. The school secretary, still the battleaxe who had excluded me on my first day at school, had played tennis for Yorkshire in her younger days and was particularly assiduous in guarding the school's reputation. She was often to be seen marching purposefully across the boggy field which separated 'the wall' from the far side of the tennis courts, shouting at the distant figures by the road. As she drew nearer they would inevitably disperse and she would advance on individuals, flailing imaginary tennis rackets, threatening dire repercussions.

It was a mystery to me how Vicky had ever met George. Ron and me had successfully negotiated innumerable King Ted's dances without ever having to speak to anybody. But it was well known that George had the looks, as well as having brains, so his friends could be relied upon to have some attractions. I had already worked out that putting a dozen young people of both sexes into the space of an average living room was likely to lead to an element of conversation. Could this be the cure I was looking for? In the event, all my fears that George's friends might turn out to be miniature Douglas-Homes proved mercifully groundless. We were all there for exactly the same reason and it had nothing to do with the Conservative Party. A roomful of would-be Labour voters all went home with little blue membership cards and a couple of crucial phone numbers. To this day, I would like to make it clear, it remains the only thing which has ever made me grateful to the Tories.

For my Dad, who had been observing my crippling teenage shyness with increasing bewilderment, the entire event was a source of much wry humour. It had taken him at least two minutes to work out why I was going. But, as a committed Labour voter, he was determined to embarrass me as much as he could about the politics of it all. 'I hope you're not going to bring any little blue membership cards back into this house, Susan,' he kept saying, with a studied frown, or, 'Dear me, my daughter in the Young Conservatives, I thought I'd brought you up respectably!' However ridiculous it made me feel it was impossible not to laugh together, as we always did, at this latest turn of events in our family story. Except that the laughter was suddenly and dramatically stopped short the day the steel caught fire.

Wedding day, June 1948

Honeymoon in Blackpool

Starring roles at Ellesmere

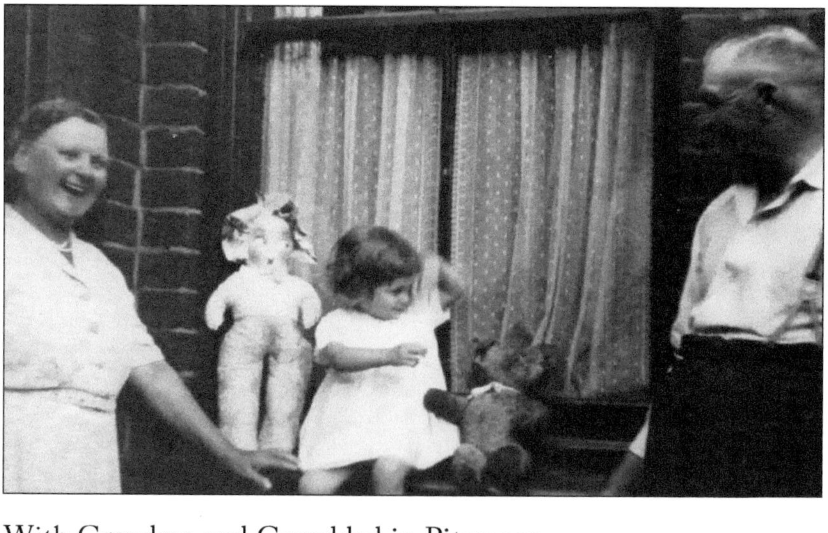

With Grandma and Granddad in Pitsmoor

The rate-fixer

Football crazy

In the garden at Gleadless Valley

A walk down Lightwood Lane

Grandma and Granddad in Pitsmoor

Working on a back-up roll in Canada

Mum in Red Square, Moscow, 1973

Working on a back-up roll in Turkey

Princess Margaret's visit to Firth Brown, 1978

The bowls champion

Celebrating the PhD

Dad on holiday in Beilstein, Germany

26

'You wouldn't think steel could burn like that...'

My Dad loved the Firth Derihon years but, just like his spell of managing the Light Machine Shops, they didn't last for long. In the event it all ended just as it had started with an episode of head-hunting. Firth Brown's directors approached him once again, asking him to move back, with a view in due course, to taking over the running of the Heavy Machine Shops.

He had very mixed feelings about returning. He knew he was going to miss the pleasures of Derbyshire and the rewards of being 'a big fish in a small pond', as he would often remark himself. But then, Firth Brown's Heavy Machine Shops, if you were in special steels at all, were the jewel in the crown, a challenge of an entirely different magnitude. If I had been overawed by the scale of operations in the Light Machine Shops as a small child, the Heavy Machine Shops were in another league altogether. Taking on the management of work on this scale would have been a major undertaking in any circumstances. But, as things turned out, he had only been in charge for five minutes, as it seemed, when the challenge began to look like a disaster. In a catastrophic conflagration, the entire lot went up in smoke.

The damage was incredible. 'You wouldn't think steel could burn like that,' people said in their stunned incredulity at the extent of the wreckage. My Dad was aghast. Not only would he be in charge of sorting out the mess he would also be expected to keep at least some of the show on the road. All through the winter that followed they kept on working, turning out what orders they could, replacing machines, in a machine shop which had no roof. It was like a scene from World War II, people said, except of course that, in Sheffield at least, the factories had never gone through anything like this. The abrupt change in working temperature affected the processing of the steel in a way which had not been foreseen, as my Dad recorded in his notebook under the prosaic title 'Cold weather drill (Shrinking)'. 'After the fire in 3/4 Machine Shops in July 1969, the first really cold weather occurred in November 1969 whilst the contractors were working on the roof and the screens at the side of the building. Temperatures recorded in the shop, at the same time of day, varied from 2 Centigrade (34 Fahrenheit) to 11 Centigrade (53 Fahrenheit). It was during this period that Greenwood made an error in grinding an Arbor to the extent of about 0.003", when it was found that the Pin from the Tool Room was also very cold, it appeared to be having the effect of making the error worse, eg. 0.006".' A description followed of lengthy discussions with Dr. F. Jones on determining the sizes of Sleeves and Arbors and agreement as to how to proceed. 'Dr Jones gave us an Electron Thermometer which gives an instant reading of temperature and is extremely useful.'

If the notebook suggests that the only problem was what was happening to the steel, memories of this affair were rather different. As one of my Dad's friends who worked in a different part of the firm recalled in horror, 'Oh, the winter! I used to go down under sufferance, under all sorts of protective clothing. However they worked there I don't know.' My Dad, without an ounce of spare fat, had always felt the cold very badly. He would walk in at night, his face burnt red from the icy wind, his eyes staring in exhaustion, his hands too cold to touch, and stand in his overcoat and hat in front of the fire, slowly trying to thaw out. Yet, when the freezing temperatures had become no more than an unpleasant memory, it was always the impact on his Machine Shops that dominated my Dad's assessment of this calamity. 'It was the best thing that could have happened,' he always said. The fire forced the firm to reinvest, to buy sparkling new machines that could operate with far greater efficiency. By the time the re-equipment of the shop was complete my Dad was in charge, in his own estimation, of 'the best and biggest machine shop in Europe'. Not just any old jewel, but a glittering diamond, in Firth Brown's crown. Unfortunately, by the time the Heavy Machine Shops had risen from the ashes, I was no longer on the spot to see for myself just what had been achieved.

27

'Don't let me catch you drinking in pubs...'

Where does it end, the intense and effortless love between fathers and daughters? If it runs on, strong and powerful like a constant presence behind our every action in our adult years, it seems to become, more often than not, unspoken. The words are lost because there is too much to say. Because a toddler's love, so massive and unquestioning in the years when Daddy fills the sky, seems inappropriate and embarrassing in the mouth of a grown woman. There is an awkwardness in this discovery, when the inevitable separation of the teenage years seems impossible to breach. Perhaps it is different now but in those days the gulf between the worlds which men and women inhabited was very wide. Somewhere in our growing up our fathers stepped aside, distanced themselves physically when things started to get messy, leaving our mothers to sort out the bits that were unmentionable, and us to pretend that nothing was happening because, of course, it was unthinkable to refer to the changes taking place. But steadily, inexorably, the relationship changed. For my Dad and me it became more cerebral, perhaps, more considered, more ironic, with the loss of physical closeness disguised by debate, discussion and the endless recounting of stories from work or school. And the circle of separation would finally close with the inevitable appearance of 'the boyfriend'.

I remember my Dad's quiet rage when I returned home one night in tears at being stood up on a first date by a boy who couldn't be bothered to trudge through the snow to meet me. I remember him searching for me and Ron in his car, anxious and angry that we were late back from the youth club because we'd finally been brave enough to find some boys to talk to. I remember his carefully-set deadlines for return from parties and rock concerts. I had immense leeway and could have been getting up to anything. But I wasn't, because he trusted me. I could never have thrown that back in his face. This mutual negotiation extended to things my friends regarded as idiotic trivialities.

My father had a thing about under-age drinking and noted with disapproval the regular lists of offenders appearing before the magistrates which were printed in the Sheffield Star. 'Don't let me catch you drinking in pubs, Susan', he'd say, 'I don't want to see my name in t'paper.' The idea that such a thing might be possible - something so awesomely unrespectable - filled me with constant dread and fuelled what my friends saw as an incomprehensible love of bitter lemon. I became a connoisseur of the different brand names, of the thickness of the lemon slice, the shape of the glass. Sometimes I'd have a double bitter lemon for a treat. On my eighteenth birthday, when my boyfriend came back from the bar with a double of my favourite tipple, his face was a picture of slow-dawning realisation when I sent him back for a lager. 'I always thought you liked this stuff,' he said.

If the separation was carefully measured when I was still at school and always took account of my Dad's concerns and preoccupations the same could not be said of life once I got to university. Though it had not been at all clear to me, even as I was approaching A Levels, that this would be a direction I would be able follow. Nobody in my family had a secondary education. A Levels were completely uncharted territory. Sticking with my childhood obsessions I had chosen to study all the foreign languages available to me and had been rewarded with a gigantic stroke of luck. Suddenly, as I approached the sixth form, the school acquired a new teacher of German who turned out to have a degree in Russian. Kate Wheeldon began at once to offer Russian classes, something I had been hoping to encounter since I was six and Dad had turned up with the globe from Woolworths. The language was everything

I had always hoped it would be: a mystical alphabet to learn to write, verbs which were cunningly indistinguishable from each other, grammatical concepts of dizzying complexity. I loved every minute of it, was entranced by the wonderful writings of Chekhov, Dostoevsky and Tolstoy we soon began to explore. Above all, learning with Kate was an absolute joy. As I was the only person in my year who wanted to study A Level I had hours of Kate's patient tuition all to myself. She was unfailingly kind and generous with her time, a gifted teacher who became a valued friend. Suddenly, studying this tricky language and visiting this enigmatic land with its rich and fascinating culture actually became a real possibility.

But I had absolutely no confidence that I would be good enough to gain a university place. My Dad had no such doubts, though he was always very guarded in what he said – he was determined that no daughter of his would end up being a bighead. His concerns about my future were of a rather different order. He insisted on sending me off to the Youth Employment Office to do all their vocational testing. He wanted me to find out whether university was really right for me, whether it would suit me as a person, not just as someone who could pass exams. Afterwards, in the throes of A Level revision, he was forever trying to make sure that the schoolwork did not cause me undue stress. He would come and drag me out of the room where I was toiling over my homework and say, 'right, that's enough for tonight, come and watch Z Cars, come and have a laugh at Morecambe and Wise.' I always blessed him for this in later life when I realised just what he had done. How special is it for anyone to know that they are loved and valued for the person they are, not for what they have achieved?

Oddly enough, it was steel which directed me to the fall-back position. I had always loved the Mappin gallery in Weston Park where Dad would guide me around the Sheffield plate and cutlery to marvel at the Norfolk knife - the magnificent array to which the Master Cutler would add a knife each year. It was whilst walking around one of the Mappin's end-of-year shows by the local art students, admiring the shining teapots and silver jewellery, that it occurred to me to take my impending Art A Level (strangely, it had never crossed my mind that I might fail that one) to the city's Silversmithing Diploma course. It seemed to be the nearest thing to keeping the family tradition that I could think of. Somehow, and without the slightest experience of it, there was an absolute certainty in the back of my mind that working with metal would be an entirely natural and comfortable thing to do.

But, in the event, the languages were enough to take me away from home, if only, at first, to nowhere more exotic than West Yorkshire. Our headmistress was singularly unimpressed by my choice of universities. In a school where it was taken as read that Oxford and Cambridge were the only answer for anyone serious about their education my selection of Bradford clearly appeared nothing if not perverse. 'Bradford ... mmm ...' she said, peering exasperatedly at me over the rim of her spectacles, 'yes, well, they seem to get on with their work there.' In an age of student unrest, of demonstrations and sit-ins by students all across Europe, this was evidently the kindest thing she could think of to say for the place. I said nothing. It seemed a complete waste of time to explain that someone like me expected to have to work for a living. I needed practical skills, professionally taught. And Bradford offered a much sought-after contemporary language course, with translation and interpreting, politics and economics, the foundation I was sure I would need. Nor was I prepared to share with her the best of all: that this was the only place in the country to have a direct exchange with a university in the USSR, that if I worked hard enough I might finally get to visit my secret place of 'forest and bears'.

It was probably just as well that I didn't try to explain. For what I could never have said was that, after seven years in a school which always made me feel as if I had crashed the wrong party, even a redbrick university, never mind Oxbridge, had seemed impossible to contemplate. It was such a relief to find myself at Bradford, where the social science library hummed gently to the strains of pop music wafting up from the ice rink below, where the lecture rooms looked out on the panorama of Chester Street bus station and where the evening's entertainment invariably included a raucous 'Zulu Warrior' from a horde of drunken student engineers. I used to watch them, lager in hand, trying to imagine the High School's reaction. For me, it was the perfect finishing school.

But if Bradford rescued me from the 'original comprehensive school' it also let me off the leash, away from my Dad's carefully concerned eye. Midway through my first term it struck me that being unrespectable might lead to having a very good time indeed. I had landed, quite suddenly, in a world where going around shouting seemed quite normal. There were student demos marching into the city centre, shouting at Maggie Thatcher. There were noisy discos where everyone yelled out the chorus of Rod Stewart's 'Maggie May'. Loud clothes and louder music were the order of the day. It seemed that 'drawing attention to yourself', far from being scandalous, was suddenly the thing to do. I was enthralled. And so, having quickly discarded the first rule of behaviour for the 'respectable-working-class', I now decided that, in this liberated age of the early 1970s, none of it any longer needed to apply to me.

28

'Unfit to be a teacher...'

Somewhere in my second term at Bradford I made a new friend on my course, someone with whom I could talk endlessly and fascinatingly. Luckily, I thought, he didn't attract me at all, wasn't my type in the least. And then, suddenly and mysteriously, one night at a party, everything changed. And that was it. The chaotic, headlong tumbling into complete inseparability which followed seemed exhilarating, terrifying and totally unstoppable, like the big wheel you can't get off no matter how much your stomach lurches until, at last, the music comes to an end.

At the end of our first year Steve and I both got holiday jobs in Yarmouth serving the tourist trade and saving money for a round-Europe trip with an Interrail ticket and a tent in September. We began by living in at our respective places of work. Steve had a very pleasant, neat, quilted and vallanced twin room shared with a fellow waiter in the basement of a seafront hotel. But responding to a job advert in the Sheffield Star from a Cypriot-owned restaurant ('Today's Special - Steak Pie and Chips, 33 pence', it said, every day) was somewhat less successful. We were allocated beds in a bare-boarded attic of three spartan rooms where, very soon, no less than fifteen girls were sharing a single toilet and bath. As more temporary waitresses arrived to boost our numbers I just couldn't stand it. Steve and I had already planned to find a place to live together in Bradford for our second year. Maybe we should just bring our plans forward a bit?

We saw an advert for a room at the cheap end of Yarmouth, rang the landlord and raced down to the jewellers for an inexpensive silver band which might pass muster as a wedding ring. In those days no self-respecting landlord, as far as we knew, was likely to rent a room to an unmarried couple. We duly turned up to view the room as the highly respectable 'Mr. and Mrs. Jones', a hard-working student couple, late of the catering trade. We soon realised that the landlord was not remotely interested in our marital status provided his five pounds per week (each! - I only earned eleven pounds basic!) turned up without fail when he paid his visit every Thursday evening. We soon found out why, when a tour of the kitchen and sitting room revealed half the lacquered and mascara-ed dance troupe from the end of the pier show and the various gentlemen they entertained. Upstairs, a genuinely married couple of professional singers constantly and vainly tried to raise the tone. Coming upon me once in the communal kitchen separating eggs to make a chocolate mousse, the only dessert I knew, which Kate had taught me, the wife decided to take me under her wing. Ever afterwards she would offer little gems of culinary advice to keep my 'hubby' happy and loved to moan about the low standards to be expected in Britain in general, and Yarmouth in particular. 'I do think it is <u>such</u> a shame that you can't find fresh tarragon anywhere in this country like you can in France. Don't you dear?'

Towards the end of August, as tips from increasingly efficient waitressing were getting heavier and heavier in my apron pocket each day and we were ever more settled into comfortable coupledom, my parents suddenly announced during my weekly phone call one night that they thought they'd call and visit me. They were going to take my grandparents to Skegness. I flew into a panic. 'It's a long way to drive from Skegness,' I said, solicitously. 'It's all right, we'll enjoy the ride,' they said. They were adamant. I didn't know what to do. They'd be bound to want to come back to the flat if they were there for the day. Perhaps I should get Steve to leave, hide all his things. But the room was obviously too big and expensive with its huge double bed which would make it glaringly clear I wasn't 'sharing with a friend'. I thought of a million excuses but none of them seemed to work. In the end I thought, well, I've always told them the truth, I've always been able to talk to them. This is what I should do now. And in it, no doubt, lay also an element of bravado: I'm grown up now. It's my life. I'm not a child any more.

Not a child, maybe. But certainly in that state of selfish intoxication which makes new lovers peculiarly dense about other people's feelings. When I rang them next, allowing an interval for delivery of the fateful letter, they were still speaking to me. And, to their eternal credit, were still planning to come to Yarmouth. I have no idea what I had wrought in their neat and quiet house, though I got some inkling of it later when Mum showed me the tablets for anxiety she'd been prescribed by the doctor. I was shocked to see how upset she was but it didn't change my position. It seemed so easy to be self-righteous, to be pig-headed, to revel in how 'modern' I was being. These were revolutionary times and I was a university student, I was in the vanguard now.

Yet these were the days when 'nice girls' didn't have sex before marriage. Or, if they did, they certainly didn't advertise it by moving in with their boyfriends. The contraceptive pill could only be obtained by running a gauntlet of moralising doctors who, at the very least, expected you to be engaged and, preferably, within a month or two of the wedding day. Abortion had only recently ceased to be a criminal offence and an unwanted pregnancy was still something to be feared for the appalling social stigma it brought. It seems unimaginable now but just before I arrived in Bradford an incident occurred which illustrates precisely the climate of the times. A girl had been thrown out of the teacher training college right next to this very university when her boyfriend was discovered in her halls of residence room. Her attempt to be reinstated led all the way to the High Court where Lord Denning pronounced her 'unfit to be a teacher' and the screaming national newspaper headlines destroyed whatever shreds of a reputation she had left. The 'swinging sixties' had been and gone but the mood beyond London's Carnaby Street and Abbey Road had scarcely been touched. Wedding rings and promises of serious commitment were the essential prelude to sexual activity in most provincial towns. We still lived in a land where thousands of pregnant girls disappeared from view each year in silent shame until their babies could be handed over for adoption.

If this was the national climate, what did my behaviour look like in a household which had a morbid fear of being caught with a half of lager? Whatever the answer, my parents arrived in Yarmouth and tried to be warm and loving to me, polite and courteous to Steve. They took us out for lunch and we all tried hard to make pleasant conversation. Afterwards, in a wild stab at normality, I decided to take some snaps. One of them, even now, makes me catch my breath. They are standing on a bridge, all three: Mum is laughing, nervously, Steve is standing in his tie-dyed T-shirt looking pensively towards the water, and my Dad? Well, my Dad couldn't quite bring himself to look into the camera at all. He is leaning heavily on the railings, staring fixedly over the edge, permanently caught in Kodachrome, turning away.

29

'The jewel in the crown...'

By the time I set off for the year abroad at the heart of my languages degree my parents and I had, to all intents and purposes, re-established full diplomatic relations. However upset they both were at my brazen and, in their eyes, foolhardy, behaviour, they were not going to let it wreck the friendship we had always shared. In my second year at Bradford, Steve and I moved in together into a surprisingly tidy house shared with three other guys from our course. My parents, to their immense credit, dealt with this development with their customary sang froid. Only occasionally did they betray their real feelings. Once, when my mother was describing the girls I'd been at primary school with all getting married and having babies, she said, 'I never know what to say about you.' And I could hear in her voice the longing for normality to share with her friends, instead of the unmentionable situation she was lumbered with. Another time, in my grandparents' dark terrace back in Pitsmoor, Grandma suddenly came out with, 'Are they nice girls you share with?' and my father's face took on the look it had reserved years earlier in Paignton for the flying fried egg. 'Mmm,' I had murmured, weakly, hearing the ghostly buckets and spades clanking all around the room.

Just as I left Sheffield for university my Dad hit the peak of his career. He was now in his late forties, running the 3/4 Machine Shops, 'the jewel in the crown' at Firth Brown. Away from home, I no longer had the unremarkable, day in, day out descriptions of events or the overheard conversations and phone calls to tell me about his working life. Just as importantly, I became immersed in my own affairs, in the excitement of university, the joys and miseries of relationships, the demands of my own world of work. My Dad's concerns, though still ever present, seemed now to be at one remove. So it was only many years later, when he was no longer with us, that I realised just how much I had missed. Why, I was forever thinking, do we never ask the questions when we can still get the answers? Why do we always leave it too late? But there were still some clues to be found to what happened at Firth Brown.

One day, my Mum brought Dad's old briefcase down from the spare bedroom. Its contents begged as many questions as they answered. There were books and books full of calculations and descriptions of processes, handbooks of steel specifications and Firth Brown products, pages photocopied or cut out of specialist magazines with titles such as 'Machining Nimonic'. There was a fifty-foot rule, an eyeglass and a whole collection of slide rules, including his own from the rate-fixing days with machine speeds marked on it. 'Look at this,' I remembered him saying, 'it's completely unique. We made our own because you couldn't buy a slide rule with what we needed on it. I ought to donate this to a museum!' There was a stamp with his signature etched into it, the huge, swirling, capital F absolutely unmistakable as his.

Then there were the photographs, some taken for publicity, some taken as evidence when jobs had gone wrong or accidents had happened, all neatly inscribed on the back with their descriptions:

'Cylinder for Canadian Power Station', with a man inside it, measuring;

'Sixty foot long "Walking Shafts", four per machine used in opencast mining';

'M.O.D. (Naval) Yoke for nuclear submarine. Part of elevator equipment to determine angle of dive.'

'Sixty-five ton Back up Rolls used in rolling mills throughout the world';

'Eccentric cylinder for paper producing machinery', a huge and intriguing structure this, with spherical and elliptical holes cut into the sides of a cylinder with changing diameters, all machined from one piece of steel.

There were so many things here that I knew something about, only nothing seemed quite enough. What I needed were some eyewitnesses.

Derek Taylor had come to my Dad's funeral, supporting himself on his stick, breathing heavily, with the oxygen cylinder, as always, in the back of his proudly luxurious car. My Dad had expressed concern about Derek's poor health for ages. 'Frank always expected that I would be the first to "cross the bar", to coin a naval euphemism, and I totally agreed with that,' Derek had written in his magnificently illegible handwriting after the funeral, 'so it was a great, tragic shock when he rang me that evening not all that long ago to tell me his terrible news.' I had asked him if I could talk to him about their days at Firth Brown. What came back, wonderfully unexpectedly, was 'An appreciation of Frank Allott', with a dictaphone tape to accompany what he suspected would be beyond anyone's power to decipher. As I made my way through it, listening to his voice, the row of question marks in my head began, at least a little, to recede.

Derek was a research chemist, based not in the machine shops of Firth Brown but in the Brown Firth research laboratories. Their paths had crossed after he had been made manager of the Works Liaison Department. 'This was the background when Frank and I first met,' he wrote. 'Frank had progressed to become the Manager of the 3/4 (Heavy) Machine Shops and if anyone thought that would be some kind of a sinecure they would be sadly mistaken. The Light Machine Shops had problems, of course, but generally in speed and throughput. Piece work (on which Frank could justly claim to be an expert) in those shops was a matter of 'how many and how quickly'. The problems in the Heavy Machine Shops were vastly different and needed a man of Frank's vast experience and calibre to face and solve them.

'The machine tools in the 3/4 Machine Shops were monster affairs, capable of machining bits of steel up to fifteen to twenty tons, fifteen to twenty feet long and several feet in diameter. They had to be planned into long-term programmes (several weeks were common or even the rule), so that just receiving a piece into the Shops had to be integrated with the time the machine tool, or tools, would be available to deal with it. The matter of availability of shop floor space was a particularly difficult headache. It was something our lords and masters seemed either to disregard or - more likely, we thought, in our moments of cynicism - something about which they were totally ignorant. On top of that was the calculation of the speed of turning, the correct cutting tool to be used, having regard to the variables surrounding the quality of steel being machined, the depth of cut - innumerable factors. You and I would stand aghast with dismay at even having to solve the equation. Then there were the measurements.'

As Derek warmed to his theme, he began listing a staggering array of technical items which were simply part of daily life in the Heavy Machine Shops: 'the inside and outside micrometers up to four to five feet in diameter, the slip gauges and length bars to calibrate them, verniers and vernier calipers, all of which had to be calibrated to National Physical Laboratory standards and at agreed frequencies. And there were both Imperial and Metric instruments for all these devices. One of the jobs I was given was to organise calibration, company-wide, and including the Glasgow works (another satellite which Frank looked after in his 'spare time') which embraced all the company's measuring equipment. It may be of interest to name the main items: Tensile Testing Machines, Bend Testing Machines, Izod and Charpy Machines, Fatigue and Creep Testing Machines, Pyrometers, Bench Potentiometers for measuring them, Portable Potentiometers, Temperature Recording, Control and Indicating Machines for Heat Treat and Melting Furnaces, Vacuum Gauges, Weights, Weighing Bridges, Scales. The list goes on and on. But at the very top for sheer volume were

Dimensional Measuring Instruments of which there is a variety you'd hardly find credible. There were over 4000 such instruments in Sheffield Works alone, and about a quarter of them, the biggest and most difficult of them all for calibration purposes, were in 3/4 Machine Shops.'

I was delighted with all the technical details. It didn't seem to matter that I had no idea what most of these things were. The important part was in Derek's confirmation of the complexities of the life of the Heavy Machine Shop. Things I knew only anecdotally, snippets of information I could never quite string together, began in this and in the remainder of the piece he had written to make more sense. I decided to go and see Derek, tape recorder in hand.

30

'It's like your mother's cake...'

What interested me most of all was something my Dad had talked about many times: the production of back-up rolls. Yet what I actually understood of the processes involved I could have written on the back of a postcard. Rolling mills worldwide, I knew, rolled their plate or sheet steel through hardened steel rolls to produce the panels for car bodies, fridges, beer and soft drink cans. But these rolls, in turn, needed back up rolls to give them strength. The back-up rolls were huge, maybe three feet in diameter, but were much more than simply a very large piece of rolled steel. So what were they exactly?

'You know, when you think about it,' Derek said, over the pub lunch he'd invited me to, 'it's a terribly interesting thing this. They didn't make back up rolls entirely out of the steel that was desirable to come into contact with the hardened steel rolls. They had a ductile centre and then you shrunk the sleeves on of the right quality, and that's quite a delicate business. And the biggest skill of all is calculating the clearances and the temperatures that you need. You see, what you do is machine the sleeve and the core - I can't remember what it's called, we'll call it the core - what you had to do was heat the sleeve so it expanded and then it would drop down on the core and it would shrink and be a shrink-fit, it's an interference fit actually, that's the correct term. But you don't want it to contract too much otherwise the forces would split it. On the other hand, if it doesn't contract enough it will slip off. And that was the crucial point in calculating the precise diameters of the outside of the core and the inside of the sleeve. The sleeves were three per cent chrome moly-vanadium and they'd to be hardened quite nicely.'

Derek's reminiscences sent me back to my Dad's old briefcase. There, in a blue hardback foolscap notebook with a handwritten contents list of twenty-seven processes, were the procedures for back-up rolls including the word 'arbor', the term for 'core' that Derek had been unable to remember. 'It's like your mother's cake,' my Dad would sometimes say to people he met in later life who knew nothing of steel-making, and the style of the notes were indeed exactly like a recipe book.

'<u>**Deshrinking Sleeves**</u>
Deshrink by Gas rings set horizontally around Sleeve at 1" apart, each ring has approximately 80 1/8" holes. May be from 0" to 8" gap between rings and Sleeve, ideal gap would be 4"-5", but nearest ring has to be used. Temperature raised is approx. 550/600 degrees centigrade, usually Sleeve drops off around 1½ hours approx, have been known to take three hours, and on odd occasions two attempts needed. About 60 lbs Air pressure is used with the gas to produce a blue flame.

<u>**Shrinking Sleeves**</u>
Usually done on a 48 hour cycle, but can be done in 24 hour cycle when required, as follows.
At 4pm put Sleeve in Furnace.
At 8am insert Arbor in Sleeve.
At 3pm (7 hours) remove Arbor and Sleeve.
Between 3pm and 4pm put in next Sleeve.'

Instructions as prosaic as these suggest almost a commonplace activity and give few hints of the magnitude of what was involved. Yet these 'recipes' were for jobs on an enormous scale.

A description of the largest sleeve and arbor ever produced in 3/4 Machine Shops is dated 1969 and refers to a job some twenty-three feet in length and weighing sixty-nine tons. Beneath this, in my Dad's hand, is written, 'above information refers to time when only seventy ton crane available in 4 Machine Shop.' Subsequently, the notebook describes test lifts in 1976-7 with a new seventy-five ton crane. 'Can now shrink a bigger combined Sleeve and Arbor than indicated in 1969,' my Dad has written, 'Bob Jennings stated "can get another 4" if absolutely necessary".' The sheer scale of work in the Heavy Machine Shops was a constant consideration when attempting to improve production and meant that technical advances might simply be inappropriate for the massive jobs involved.

In 1970, for example, my Dad went to Stafford to attend a demonstration of high speed grinding. In the blue notebook he set out what he had seen and listed its advantages. Then he observed, 'snag as far as No.3 concerned, to get best results, it is essential that Work speed as well as Wheel speed is twice the normal, does not look practical with our size and weight of job.' The stock-in-trade of the Heavy Machine Shops was the combination of massive scale with pinpoint accuracy, as the drawings and notes and observations such as, 'customer will not accept any rolls outside tolerances' constantly emphasise. A classic example of this are the drawings of propellor shafts for nuclear submarines to be delivered to Vickers Ltd., fifty-one feet in length, with calculations as to how to accommodate this in the shop by making some physical adjustments to the premises. 'Inside and outside diameters to be perfectly concentric,' the drawing states, 'shaft to be statically balanced before dispatch'. And there are pages and pages of calculations in my Dad's handwriting to achieve this end.

Meanwhile, behind all of these technical problems, ran the day to day questions of pay and conditions for the operators on the machines. A workplace of such complexity, where jobs were frequently 'one offs', did not readily lend itself to a broad-brush approach to improving efficiency. It was a factor which he felt the work study 'experts', periodically drafted in by the directors, often had difficulty grasping. With his unparallelled knowledge of rate-fixing, my Dad's notes reveal him taking issue with schemes proposed by management consultants, demonstrating the errors in their calculations and concluding that the systems they propose will de-motivate rather than encourage: 'these work values will deter operators from improving their performance of their own free will'. One of my Dad's most well-thumbed books on the shelf at home was a weighty black-bound tome entitled 'Payment by Results'. He was determined to be equipped to beat the consultants at their own game. 'What is the Alternative?' is the heading of a report he authored in which he looked in depth at failures in the implementation of the existing piece work scheme: 'I am in favour of a Work Study Based Piecework scheme. The main weakness of the existing system in my opinion is that we have no facility or organisation to follow up a calculation.'

His proposals also took a long look at accepted working practices: 'We have been content in the past, mainly due to lack of qualified Staff, to accept that if a man had done a job piecework, then that was sufficient, accepting perhaps returns of five shillings per hour when possibly seven shillings could have been earned. Progress could be made if an operator was told which tools to use. For too long we have accepted the mainly passive role of the Foreman, whose duties seem to consist of signing Work Cards, irrespective of what is written on them, or making sure that a queue doesn't form at the clock five minutes before finishing time.' As for the London-based consultants, their report had clearly rattled him, and not merely for the potentially-damaging consequences of their proposals, as his parting shot revealed: 'Appendix IV wants rewriting so it can be understood, preferably in English.' All of the knowledge my Dad had acquired, of technical processes, work study and management, had come together in the running of the Heavy Machine Shops. Now, in an effort to secure Firth Brown's continuing competitiveness, it was about to take him transatlantic.

31

'We ought to go out there, change our lives...!'

Travelling abroad on business was a prospect my Dad had never envisaged and one which, at first, he thoroughly relished. Firth Brown supplied steel to twenty-five countries but overseas competition was ever increasing. The idea now was that foreign companies would continue to order steel from Firth Brown in return for being shown how to resolve the problems inherent in producing back up rolls. My Dad was to be entrusted with the task of supervising operations overseas. It could scarcely have begun in a more pleasant manner with a trip to the steel mills at Hamilton, Ontario - though North America seemed much further away in 1973. I was in the middle of my degree course on a work-experience placement as a translator in Paris when he set off. 'Arrived OK,' the postcard said, 'after a thirteen-hour air journey, in the same seat on the same plane, Manchester – Glasgow – Montreal - Toronto. Very tiring.'

Things improved once on site as the work itself went triumphantly well after an inauspicious beginning, as my Dad explained in his report. 'The first situation which was not to my liking was as follows. The furnace and the Roll Sleeves had been installed in the Maintenance Shop, the Arbors were to be ground in the Roll Grinding Shop, a distance of two miles or so separating the two shops, even worse, the shops are under two separate supervisors ... Before the Sleeves were dispatched to Dofasco, it was their intention to grind the Arbors to sizes supplied by Firth Brown. I requested that they did not grind until I arrived, and it was extremely fortunate that this step was taken, as their method of grinding and more particularly their method of measuring was far removed from the standard required. However I was able to exert my influence on the foreman and the grinding machine operators so that by the time the third Arbor had been ground they were grinding and measuring in a manner which was acceptable to me, and they are under no illusions that these standards must be maintained in future.'

Attached to his report on the visit was a lengthy explanation of the procedures to be followed once the people in Hamilton were left to their own devices. Eight copies of this were duly dispatched to Canada and are notable not merely for the technical detail but for what they reveal about the delicacy of this operation to unite the sleeve and arbor of a back-up roll. 'Presume Arbor has been ground satisfactorily and Sleeve has been in furnace sixteen hours minimum at 250 degrees Centigrade (482 degrees Fahrenheit). ... Arbor can then be hoisted into a vertical position, care being taken to ensure that the Arbor is hanging vertically by using a Vertical Spirit Level, the bottom six inches of the Arbor to be oiled to make entry easier. Lift off Furnace top, replace by standing platform. Sleeve should be straw coloured. Pass adjustable Pin Gauge quickly to ensure expansion has taken place. Gently enter Arbor into Sleeve (care should be taken to ensure Arbor enters without bumping and also straight, any marking of the Sleeve at this stage is unacceptable and if this occurs Arbor should be removed, Sleeve and Arbor dressed and the operation of expanding the Sleeve recommenced), lower Arbor until resting in recess in Sleeve, remove outer Furnace wall and allow to contract for seven hours when it will be possible to remove combined Arbor and Sleeve from the Furnace and the procedure repeated if necessary. When the Arbor and Sleeve are removed from the Furnace no machining should be done on the Back-Up Roll for five or six days, i.e. when the Sleeve is only 'hand warm'.'

The Canadians were more than happy with the assistance they had received. Secreted inside one of the notebooks in the briefcase was an effusive testimonial written by the managing director of the Canadian firm and sent to Firth Brown whilst the work was still taking place. My Dad, with his characteristic modesty, never mentioned this at home. 'This is just a note to report to you on just what is happening in regard to Frank Allott's visit to Dofasco. The first arbor was inserted in its sleeve yesterday (Wednesday), the second one was inserted in its sleeve this morning and the third one will be inserted in its sleeve first thing tomorrow morning. His knowledge of his job is, of course, superb. The interesting thing to me is the really magnificent way that he has worked with everybody at Dofasco. He has been able to get them to come around to his thinking in regard to the accuracy needed, when they were not so inclined, without in any way ruffling any feathers. Everybody with whom he has dealt is tremendously impressed with him and, because of his own manner and attitude, have given him tremendous cooperation. I am just delighted with not only Frank himself but with the job that he is doing here and with the results that he is getting.' Not surprisingly, they offered him a job and, on even such a short acquaintance with Canada, he was sorely tempted.

All who were involved in facilitating his visit to Hamilton had ensured that he was made more than welcome. The weather was just right for going out in boats on Lake Ontario and his counterparts in the firm were a pleasure to spend time with. They were also, by Sheffield standards, amazingly well-off with their high salaries, their huge modern houses and their cabins and yachts on the lake. It was more than a little tempting once he realised that his skills were thoroughly in demand. 'One of them has a daughter who runs a language school,' he told me over an international phone line. 'When I told them you were in Paris she said she could use you, no problem. We ought to go out there, change our lives!' It didn't get discussed for long. Just at the point at which my Mum was getting interested he started backpedalling. It reminded me of exactly the same process a decade earlier. Every week the newspaper would carry adverts for the 'Ten Pound Passage' to Australia. For skilled men such as my Dad, just ten pounds took you and your family on the ship to Sydney where they were crying out for good workers. My Dad would go on and on about it, Mum and I would put up a spirited defence for as long as we could and then, when he'd completely worn us down, he'd say, 'What about your Grandma and Granddad though? We can't leave them and they'd never leave Sheffield.' They weren't on their own, of course. Whatever he said, it was clear as daylight that neither would he.

32

'I'm in charge of all this. Imagine...!'

The praise and respect my Dad received in Canada were regularly mirrored by now back in Sheffield. It was obvious to me on the occasions when I went home and we would bump into men from work, or other ex-referees, as we walked through the middle of town. Everyone wanted to stop and talk to him. He had a smile, a joke and a story for each one. I could see in their faces the affection and respect. It reminded me of walking with my Grandma as a child on Spital Hill: the same picture but on a larger canvas. Sometimes, the chance meetings were a bit more dramatic. I recall one time running into a man who absolutely insisted on buying my Dad a glass of beer, making a huge fuss of him until my Dad, in some embarrassment, put a stop to it. 'What was all that about?' I asked him later. He didn't want to tell me. Eventually, under some pressure from me, he described how the man had one day, without warning, climbed to the top of the highest crane in the Machine Shops and had been about to jump. My Dad had gone up there and sat with him, gradually talking him down. He had never said a word about it at home. 'He always makes a fuss, I wish he wouldn't,' was all he said.

As his work at Firth Brown turned him into a world traveller, he grew in stature and confidence. The results of this were played out in all kinds of unexpected little public incidents. On one occasion I had popped home on a flying visit from Bradford with no luggage and just the jeans and T-shirt I stood up in. My Dad decided to take us out for a posh meal. As we were about to enter the restaurant he had chosen, I spotted a discreet sign in the window: 'No jeans'. Just at this moment the manager opened the door to greet my smartly-suited father. 'I'm just looking at this notice,' he said. 'Surely you can't mean this to refer to my charming daughter here?' 'Of course, sir,' the manager said, unctuously, 'in your case, we will do you the favour of making an exception.' 'Wait a minute,' my Dad said, 'let's just be quite clear about who's doing who the favour here!'

My Mum watched all this in growing wonderment. 'He wouldn't say boo to a goose when I first knew him,' she used to say. She would describe how, on one of the occasions when he had dislocated his shoulder playing football before they were married, he had come down to her stepmother's house. With his shoulder strapped up, he couldn't fasten his shoe laces and had walked all the way back to his mother's house with them undone because he was too shy to ask his future dragon-like mother-in-law for help. 'You can't imagine it now!' my Mum used to say, shaking her head in amazement. No doubt the way he behaved by the time he was managing the Heavy Machine Shops reflected the esteem he was aware of and the pride he felt in the work he did. Derek Taylor summed it up in his characteristically carefully-chosen words: 'Frank's guidance to me was invaluable. He was a big-hearted man, generous in his help and cooperation to everyone who, without exception, admired and respected him in return.' Sometimes, my Dad would tell me, he'd sit on the steps at the end of the Shop, at the end of a working day. He'd look down the immense length of it, past the gleaming machines and the jobs in production by the 300 or more who worked there, and he'd think, 'I'm in charge of all this. Imagine!' He was still next door to the place he was born on Carlisle Street but he might as well have been a galaxy away. It was quite something for a graduate of All Saints Church of England Primary School. 'Not bad, is it, Susan?' he'd say.

And so we never went to Canada. As the seventies wore on and life at Firth Brown became very much harder I think my Dad often regretted it. In all probability, a less stressful life beside

Lake Ontario would probably have saved his health. As times got tougher I often wished I'd responded with more enthusiasm to the job at the language school. But working with French was always going to be second-best for me. It was, after all, my Dad who had set me off in my search for the land of 'forest and bears'. And, in the middle of my university year abroad, I was almost there: with a bit of luck, I could see the enigma that was Russia just up ahead of me.

33

'The hub of downtown Moscow...'

It was an ancient bus, reeking of petrol. Early October and the windows already felt like ice, and through the dismal greyness of the windows themselves, more grey beyond, stretching out endlessly on the road that led away from the Belorussian Station. A splash of green and white on a vast grey square, the station facade itself turned grey through the back window as the bus bumped and rocked along its dead straight, wide road. Someone, one of the smartly-suited young men with the puzzling American accents who had come to meet us, was using the word 'boulevard'. 'This is our central boulevard, the hub of downtown Moscow.' It was a bizarre description for a landscape so blank, made worse as it dawned on me that the student who was speaking was actually Russian. I had expected to feel excited and pleased at my new adventure. Instead, I felt only a growing sense of dismay.

There were no adverts, no multicoloured hoardings, no bright lights. Worst of all, it appeared, there were no shops. I was appalled. What on earth was I going to do for six months in a city with no shops?! Was it this that I'd reached out for, yearned for, in all the years of good behaviour at school? All the little miseries behind the summer reports - 'Susan tries hard at netball' - borne patiently for the sake of the adventure, of the exotica to come. And here it was: steel-grey, iron-grey, brown-grey, rust-grey, buildings with doorways of unimaginable, oppressive height, facades of blank, staring windows set in concrete. So they were right, after all, the Cold War warriors: this was the Soviet Union, 1973. Welcome to socialism, comrade. I stared out through the grime and tried to compose myself for six months of claustrophobia.

So this was where they led, I thought, all those years listening to my Dad preaching tolerance, noting his disapproval of the Yorkshire 'Tyke's' insularity. All the childhood years I had spent longing to follow Dieter and Anna to lands of gothic spires, and beyond to onion domes, and snow, and trios of horses pulling jingling, fur-covered sleighs, had come to this. Was this really all there was to be seen? This was Moscow, the capital of a place which no longer exists, the Union of Soviet Socialist Republics, the USSR. Back in 1973 it was a very different place from the bright and vibrant city of today. The sight that first met my eyes was a huge, bewildering disappointment. And we were to live right in the middle of it.

Behind one of the forbidding grey-stone facades of central Moscow was a student hostel where long grey corridors gave on to rooms painted a peeling pale green. Three of us shared a room with space enough between the beds and tables and cupboards to say 'excuse me' as we stood on each other's feet. Next door, conveniently placed, was a kitchen with two stoves where cockroaches wandered cheerily amongst the rubbish. The 'bathroom' for female students was two corridors away and two floors below us: four cracked sinks and four toilet bowls encrusted with filth, announcing their stinking existence long before you opened the door. There were showers - and we were lucky enough to be quite near them. The one entrance was through a door at the end of our sixth floor corridor and then down twelve flights of stairs to the bowels of the hostel. A tiled room with a wooden bench was hidden behind a heavy wooden door and led into the six open shower cubicles where naked girls in flip-flops wandered around with dripping hair. Back on the ground floor in the main body of the hostel was the only other amenity: a tiny buffet which, when not closed 'for technical reasons', offered stale pastries and, sometimes, fresh omelettes with black bread - if you could stand Lidya Vladimirovna's constant shouting as she thumped the abacus beads up and down their wires in between pouring tea. Well...! I had wanted to see and experience something different, something unusual, something completely unlike England. And my every wish had been fulfilled. We sat on our beds that first evening, almost shellshocked, certainly with our spirits sinking fast - until, quite suddenly, we began to laugh at the ludicrousness of the situation we found ourselves in. And it was the absurdities of hostel life in a Soviet city that kept us amused for much of the next six months.

But then, something happened. Late that evening we walked down to Red Square, into the chill of the October night air, into the blackness of the near-deserted streets. Underestimating the distance to the square between the facades of official buildings, along the side of GUM, the state department store, we broke almost into a run in the final minutes before the hour struck and the Kremlin chimes rang out. Bursting out of Kuibyshev Street onto the shining wet cobbles of Red Square we were struck dumb.

At the far side a silent crowd gathered, dark in hats and overcoats, before the glowing marble mausoleum inscribed with the one word, LENIN. Behind them rose the red brick crenellations of the Kremlin wall, the green-domed palace with its red hammer and sickle flag flapping in the light night breeze. And, at each end of the square, overwhelming, majestic, soared the immense Kremlin towers with their ruby stars, the fantastic red and white of the Historical Museum and, most extraordinary of all, the bulk of St. Basil's Cathedral appearing two-dimensional in the floodlights. Where the land fell away to the river the Cathedral rose, whirling dizzily yellow and green, blue and white, red and orange, the coloured domes swirling ever upwards into the inky black of the Moscow sky. Then, as the minute hands of the Spassky tower clocks approached the hour, three great-coated soldiers emerged through the Kremlin gates, goose-stepping solemnly the length of the Kremlin wall to stand before the mausoleum. The chimes rang out their oddly discordant music as the soldiers changed places like rapid, unsmiling marionettes to stand guard for another hour of the night over the embalmed founder of the Soviet state. The crowd pressed forward silently as the guard changed and followed their progress back to the Spassky Gate, to be swallowed up once more into the heart of Soviet power.

In those moments the Square held us spellbound with its theatrical magic, with its intensely strange and mysterious beauty, its silence, its blackness, its brilliant colours. The extraordinary enchantment of my childhood ballets was here, after all; a sight all the more compelling for its concealment in the midst of the Soviet grime. And, if this was its most public face, then the private heart of Russia must still be beating somewhere. As I gazed at the drama unfolding before me, I remembered the lessons my Dad had so carefully taught me all those years before down Lightwood Lane: I only had to look. 'Make sure you don't ever stop looking,' he always said. And he was right, of course. For when you look, really look, you should always prepare to be amazed at what you find.

34

'The typical Soviet citizen...'

Grandma had been terrified of my impending trip to Russia. Whenever I talked about it - and, after all the years of anticipation, I could scarcely keep the delight out of my voice - she would react with uncharacteristic ferocity: 'I don't know what you want to go there for. Nobody else goes there. I hope I'm dead before you go off and do that.' But then, in a period of constant political tension, you could hardly blame Grandma for fearing the Cold War enemy. Our papers were full of reports of the harsh treatment meted out to any opponents of the Soviet regime, it was only five years since Soviet tanks had rolled into Czechoslovakia to suppress a popular reform movement, and diplomats from both sides were regularly expelled for spying. My Grandma was convinced that, if I once ventured beyond that forbidding 'Iron Curtain', I would never be able to get back.

All my attempts at explaining how it would give me the language practice I needed to become a top-flight interpreter cut no ice with my sensible Grandma. Nor was regaling her with descriptions of ballets and onion domes and jolly Grandfather Frost of any avail. But, once I had arrived safely and she began receiving interesting postcards with large and beautiful stamps, she completely changed her tune. Suddenly my unlikely trip became something to show off about. She thoroughly enjoyed astounding her neighbours with news of all I was seeing and doing, of the good job it was going to get me when I'd finished my studies. The best bit, for her, came at Christmas with her golden wedding - she and Granddad had got married at 8.30am on Christmas Day 1923 - and the arrival of five huge golden chrysanthemums which I had fixed up with a florist on Ecclesall Road before I left. She loved to tell the story of how she had bemused the delivery girl by exclaiming, 'Oh, they've come from Russia!' She would laugh and dab her eyes with her pinny: 'she must have thought I'd gone mad!'

But the prospect of this first journey on the east-bound train, across the flat, empty plains of Poland, the undulating green expanse of Belorussia ('look, there aren't any hedges or walls in these fields!'), the endless, aching vistas of birch and pine as we pulled onward and onward into Russia itself, had captured the imagination of my entire family. Before I left, Mum and Dad had decided, much to my amazement, that they would pay me a visit. It shouldn't have surprised me really; my Dad had none of his mother's horror at my departure. More to the point, the fact that this was the height of the Cold War and relations between our two countries were at the lowest possible ebb only added to his determination to see for himself. With his moderate Labour Party politics my Dad had no time for Communism, but he thought that ideological differences were no excuse for a lack of diplomacy. 'In the end, politicians always have to talk to each other,' he was fond of observing, and he deplored the fact that this so often only happened when too many lives had been lost.

My Dad had lost his youth to war. He knew at first hand the fear, the darkness, the anxiety. He had seen bombing, death, homelessness, crippled lives, wretched poverty when he was still in his teens. He had endured the difficult and cheerless years which followed and rejoiced at what were, for him, the riches of a simple, peaceful life in a steady job and a modest home. He was appalled to see that this dividend of peace was threatened throughout the 1950s and 60s by the ever-accelerating nuclear arms race between East and West. And he knew, as all his generation knew, whatever the Cold War political rhetoric, that it was only the sacrifice of the Russian people in World War Two which had made our victory possible. They, more than anyone he believed, could not possibly want to go through such a war, or worse, ever again. He wanted to go and look, to find out for himself what was hidden behind all the propaganda.

My Dad was fascinated by all the details of the journey and arrangements for my stay, and rapidly realised that my trip gave him a once-in-a-lifetime opportunity to see it all too. No doubt, after what I had just put them through in Yarmouth, the Soviet Union looked like child's play. The trouble was that, even courtesy of a Thomson's package tour, holidays in the USSR were not the same as a quick trip to Germany. For some reason which I never fathomed Mum had ended up applying for and collecting their visas from the Soviet Consulate herself. Having barely ventured out of Sheffield on her own, there she was on the train to London, taking a taxi to Kensington Palace Gardens, braving the intimidating stares of the 'squat little men in dark suits', as she put it, who presided over the Consulate's entrances and exits. In the process, she provided the family's first glimpse of the unexpected humanity behind the stern facade. Handing in her form she explained that she had not filled in 'occupation' because she was 'just a housewife'. 'What do you mean, just a housewife?' the woman behind the counter had boomed in her heavily-accented English, 'That's a very important job!' she said, smiling broadly.

Even as they flew into Moscow they still had no idea what to expect. Decades of Cold War propaganda had led them to assume - and they were scarcely alone in this - that one's every move in a socialist state was subject to restriction. 'Will we be able to see our daughter?' Dad had asked the Intourist guide on the coach from the airport. 'Of course!' she had smiled, incredulous that, after a 2000-mile journey, it had seriously concerned them that they might not be allowed to see me. I was waiting in the foyer of the 'Intourist' hotel when they arrived, to their absolute delight. It was wonderful to see them, looking approvingly around the huge, modern entrance hall of the city's newest hotel, still in their coats and hats against the November cold. My Dad looked, as he so often did in winter clothing, as if he had lived in Russia all his life.

There was something about his expression and his neatness which would not have looked out of place anywhere from Moscow to Vladivostok. As a Russian friend of mine was to remark years later on seeing a photograph of him in a winter coat on the sea front at Blackpool, 'My goodness, he looks like the typical Soviet citizen!' And, in a sense, she was right.

They had an excellent week. We went sightseeing together. They would regularly wander across to the magic of Red Square on their own in the evenings where Mum fell in love with St.Basil's Cathedral and photographed it from every angle on a film which, much to her dismay, failed to process properly back home. They got tickets for me and my room-mates to accompany them to a performance of the renowned Pyatnitsky folk choir at the Tchaikovsky concert hall. We were all entranced by the strange, high harmonies in the women's voices, the fantastic colours of the outstretched sarafan skirts, the enthusiastic, rhythmic clapping of the Russians in the audience. In the middle of the week it was 7th November, the fifty-sixth anniversary of the 1917 October Revolution and they were able to watch the entire parade from the steps of their hotel. Describing it all to me later, it was not the lines of tanks or massive military hardware which had caused them to marvel. It was a far more mundane aspect of the scene: the sight of the young soldiers smoking as they waited their turn to march past the mausoleum on Red Square. 'Can you imagine getting away with that in the British army?' my Dad asked, astounded. In a similar way, they had through me a glimpse of Soviet life well beyond the smart and clean hotels for foreigners. One glance at our hostel had my Dad sacrificing his hotel lunches to me as he saw the kind of diet I was existing on.

But the thing which stayed with them the longest, which Dad talked about endlessly on his return to anyone who would listen, were the special lights on the Central Post Office building on the night of November 7th. There, on the high corner of the building, was a screen covered with light bulbs changing sequence to make pictures and words, like the old news service at Piccadilly Circus. It was telling the story of the Revolution, complete with the famous shots from the guns of a glowing red Cruiser 'Aurora', and ending with the number '56' lit up in the centre over a hammer and sickle flag. Dad would describe the crowds gathered to watch, once, twice, three times as the lights went round, with little gasps of appreciation: 'It took me right back. It was the expressions on people's faces. I could remember standing in crowds of people just like that, looking at the news in lights on the top of the 'News Theatre' in Fitzalan Square after the war. But people wouldn't do that in this country now - we've all got too sophisticated. I was fascinated watching them, seeing them behaving just the way we did twenty or thirty years ago. I quite liked that.' And so did I. It was something that attracted me too in my growing love-hate relationship with life in the USSR.

35

'A cultural exchange...'

What I loved the most, curiously enough, was the silence. The quality, which my Dad had noticed, of whole crowds of people maintaining a library-hush across an entire street is something which endured long after 1991 when the USSR finally disintegrated. Back in 1973 there were no blaring BMW horns or glaring McDonald's hoardings to interrupt the quietness. Somehow the occasional street and wall signs announcing that, 'We will bring to life the decisions of the 24th Congress of the Communist Party of the Soviet Union!' seemed to blur into the muddling quality of the November light. And, when the snow came the silence seemed total. The snow muffled everything, even the clanking of the trams and the rumbling of the ancient trolleybus wheels. Not a footfall could be heard on the narrow pavements beside the old two-storey buildings in our part of town. In the very centre, where whole districts like this had been bulldozed to usher in the Stalinist utopia, great vistas of whiteness gaped between the blank frontages of official buildings and dark figures hurried, head down, against the tumbling flakes.

I loved our part of town. I loved its old, crumbling, pastel-painted buildings, the unexpected domes of churches in backyard nooks and crannies, the giant icicles jutting from immense and battered fall pipes, the virgin snow untouched in silent courtyards which bore nothing but a fading 'watch repairs' sign. I loved it because it was so easy, here, to imagine Tchaikovsky's little swans fluttering across the ice directly out of the nineteenth century, or that the characters from Tolstoy's Anna Karenina or War and Peace would sweep around the next corner in a jingling sleigh. It was a direct link with the old, pre-revolutionary Russian culture in the novels and ballets I had fallen in love with. But it held, also, another bit of history, far more recent - the one my Dad had spotted. I loved it because it was, in so many surprising ways, like post-war Sheffield. The very sparseness which, on first glance, had repelled the seventies' trendy I thought I had become, had, with a bit more looking, revealed itself as the world of the fifties' child.

Our local Moscow shop, imaginatively entitled 'Fruit and Vegetables', enticed us inside with a display of three cabbages and two bunches of carrots arranged in a window too big for them. Within, the limited stock of cabbage, beetroot, potatoes, more cabbage and more potatoes looked to me just like Mrs. Pepperdine's shop where Grandma used to take me whenever I stayed at her house in Pitsmoor. Tumbling vegetables unwrapped into the bag you'd brought with you, expecting simplicity and finding it, seemed somehow wonderfully comforting to me. Even the grocery which proudly announced itself to be 'self-service' was full of old Sheffield tricks. Packets and bottles were not stacked high on their shelves but carefully placed, lying down in racks to conceal their scarcity. It was exactly like Woolworths after Christmas when all the biggest shampoo bottles would suddenly be too tired to stand up and would fill the huge wooden counters until the new stock came in. I knew exactly why most of my fellow students hated all of this, but I was charmed. As long as I could just wander around these streets, just looking, I was happy.

But there was, of course, a much darker side. Sometimes it expressed itself as a mere irritant in the habitual rudeness and shouting of people 'serving' in shops and cafes, behaviour which seemed all the more shocking against a backdrop of universal quietness. These naked displays of power by shop assistants, doormen, canteen workers and low-level bureaucrats spoke volumes about the system in which they were enmeshed. At the other end of the spectrum, at the very summit of the system itself, I had been horrified to discover that the Lubyanka stood only a few streets away from our hostel. The headquarters of the secret police where thousands had been tortured and murdered in the Stalin years and where the cellars, as Russian friends, with ironic exaggeration, observed, still led all the way to Siberia, stood gigantic and fearsome opposite the main children's shop on one of Moscow's central squares. Unlike every other official building it bore no signs to announce itself - and this alone made it unmistakable - it simply stood, unrepentant, as an awful warning of what Soviet power could do should it have the mind. It was as if the Nazi concentration camp of Dachau had been transported, piece by piece, replanted in the centre of Munich in 1945 and the warders reappointed with instructions to scale down their operations a touch.

Little of this, however, impinged on us as temporary visitors on a 'cultural exchange'. Aside from the everyday, unremarkable surveillance, most of the limitations and sanctions faced by our Russian fellow-students could not be imposed on us. Moreover, as a generation of British students noted for being the awkward squad, the restrictions had great potential as a game of finding out how far the bounds could be pushed. Yet for me, at least, this had much less to do with student sit-ins and demonstrations than with the mock debates and arguments that Dad and I had acted out on a Sheffield council estate many years before. Though sometimes, I soon realised, playing dumb was the only sensible tactical move to make.

36

'Getting things to your liking...'

A couple of days after our arrival Sasha turned up in our room. He was in the same year as us, he explained. He'd been asked to show us around, sort out any problems we might have. He was friendly, polite, helpful, if a little too curious about how we'd been spending our time. After this he would appear once a week and invariably bring a provocative subject with him. 'Look at this!' he would say, flinging a newspaper onto our table with some lurid photograph of Israeli atrocities, or the like. 'What do you think of that then?!' It clearly never occurred to him that this behaviour might appear bizarre in someone who was barely an acquaintance: he was carrying out instructions, after all. We would respond to this game with a game of our own. Whenever he came in with his newspaper we would each sit on our respective beds and mutter things like, 'Oh dear. Well, I don't know what to think. I've never thought about politics before, have you? No, I haven't either. Well, I don't think we've got an opinion about it. Have you heard the latest Rod Stewart record?' Sasha would become increasingly frustrated and would eventually stomp out, shouting at us to 'start reading the papers' as his parting shot. But it never stopped him coming back the following week, or watching us at public events, or snooping around our friends. He was a man on a mission.

Each little group of us in its own hostel room had its very own 'Sasha' to whom others responded a good deal more fulsomely. The 'Sashas' had a lot to gain. When that year's language exchange ran its course and the Russian students selected for the exchange arrived in London our group went down to meet them at the invitation and expense of the British Council. Imagine our delight as we walked into the Council's reception room to be met by the fond handshakes of the complete collection of 'Sashas'. Our Sasha made a beeline for us. 'Good to see you,' he beamed. 'Did you have a good journey home from the Soviet Union? Tell me, which of your Russian friends came to see you off at the station?' It was easy to play dumb with Sasha because the word 'informer' was written right through him like 'Blackpool' through rock. But it was much harder to keep your mouth shut with some of the other 'official' irritants of hostel life.

On the Wednesday of our second week a knock on the door heralded the arrival of three young men armed with clipboards who marched into the disastrous muddle of clothes, books and the remains of tea which characterised our room and proceeded to deliver their 'criticism'. We sat there open-mouthed, bread and cheese in mid-bite, as they informed us in no uncertain terms that we were untidy and unhygienic and would only score two ('unsatisfactory') out of a possible five ('excellent') this week. We had avoided a score of one ('bad') as this was our first assessment but the score would, nevertheless, be entered on the chart at the end of the corridor under the slogan, 'We are competing for the title of "Model Room"!'

So convinced were we that this was an elaborate hoax at the expense of the westerners that we sat there looking increasingly amused with each ensuing pronouncement. It was only when they slammed our door in annoyance and marched across the corridor shouting 'Sankommissiya!' - sanitary commission - at our unfortunate neighbours that we realised this was for real. Much more importantly our Russian friends weren't laughing. 'You have to put up with them. Be polite,' they said. 'They can cause you lots of trouble if they feel inclined.' We were ashamed of our naivety. Every Wednesday thereafter we would carefully clean and tidy our room then sit awaiting the 'sankommissiya', exercise books in hand. But, because we had insulted them, we were never allowed any credit for our efforts. Week after week, when much less tidy neighbours were admiring their habitual 'fives' on the 'Model Room' chart, we were scoring 'threes' or, on one particularly immaculate occasion, 'four'. When we protested and asked to be given a reason, the head clipboard announced, 'It's too hot in here', and a cynical smirk of relish at his power passed across his face. After this we reverted to normal on Wednesday evenings, not bothering to look up from our mess of tea things as they stood there, enumerating our faults. We would sit at the table saying, 'can you pass me the jam, please', or, 'shall I cut you another slice of bread?' to a background noise of the head clipboard intoning, 'crumbs on the floor, clothes not replaced in wardrobes, books on beds ...' As they left each week I took to calling after them, 'when are you going to do something about the cockroaches?' as the door slammed and the feet departed down the corridor.

The answer, apparently, was 'in time for New Year'. Huge posters appeared on the walls of each corridor announcing that a 'subbotnik', a 'voluntary working' Saturday, was to be held, organised by the 'sankommissiya', which would require everyone to give up their time to clean the hostel from top to bottom. Everyone would be assigned to a cleaning detachment in due course. They never came to us. As the day dawned we were woken by furious sounds of scrubbing in the corridor outside our room. A small army of girl students, several of them in traditional revolutionary red kerchiefs, were wielding brushes and cloths over the bare boards and skirtings along the entire floor. More girls lined the twelve flights of stairs to the showers, engaged in the crucial task of polishing the peeling handrail. Curiously enough, the male students who made up the majority of the hostel's inhabitants seemed to have disappeared for the day, with the exception of the ones with clipboards, or those mysteriously marching around, manfully carrying planks of wood. No-one was going anywhere near the cockroaches. It was clearly pointless to ask why.

Occasionally, though, challenging authority got the desired results. Early in December a notice appeared announcing that, during the week's break between semesters in January, all the hostel's foreign students were eligible to choose to tour a Soviet city whilst the Russians went home to see their families. There was Kiev, Leningrad, Volgograd, Minsk and Baku to pick from. We decided to head south for Baku - see the exotic sights of Azerbaidzhan, leave behind the Moscow snows. We were turned down flat.

'The trips aren't for you, they're for foreign students.'

'We're foreign students.'

'No, you're not, you're western students. That's different.'

I couldn't bear to let this one pass. The ensuing argument between myself and Valeri, the Komsomol (Communist Youth League) leader who had charge of all our dealings with officialdom, went on for three weeks:

'It says <u>all</u> foreign students are eligible to go to one of these five cities,' I insisted.

'Look, let me explain it to you,' came Valeri's retort, 'it means all the students from socialist countries. It means all the East Europeans, it means the Cubans, the Vietnamese, the Mongolians, the Arabs and the Africans.'

'The Arabs and the Africans don't come from socialist countries.'

'It doesn't matter. They are our comrades. Anyway, you wouldn't want to be on a trip with a load of Arabs and Africans.'

'Yes we would. We have lots of Arab and African friends back home in England. We'd be delighted.'

'Well, it's not possible.'

This, by now, was reminding me a lot of the absurd discussions about my name which had begun every year at Sheffield High School.

I went off to see the college authorities and asked very politely if we could go on a trip. We will be in the hostel all on our own. We will have no-one to practise our Russian with. We won't see any of the splendours of the USSR we've all read so much about. They relented. See Valeri, they said.

'We'd like to go to Baku, please.'

'You can't, it's not possible.'

'We've been told it is.'

'Well, it isn't. You can go anywhere but Baku.'

'Why not Baku?'

'It's too expensive to fly, and it takes too long to go by train.'

I went to the railway station and to the offices of the state airline, Aeroflot.

'It costs 32 roubles to fly. We can all afford that. And there would be time to go by train – we could do that too if necessary.'

'It's not possible. There are no tickets.'

'Yes there are. I've checked.'

Valeri came back the next day and handed each of us a ticket to Kiev. 'I expect this to keep you quiet,' he said, handing me mine. 'But you said we couldn't go anywhere,' I replied. 'How would we have got to Kiev if we hadn't asked for Baku?' By then it almost seemed a shame to go at all, we were enjoying our little game of negotiation so much, Valeri and I. I almost missed him when he didn't come to Kiev.

Thinking it over in the fogbound airport, waiting for our Kiev flight, with the Soviet leader, Leonid Brezhnev, droning away on the TV in the corner, it struck me that no-one else had said a word past the first 'oh dear'. No-one else, evidently, would have considered taking on what appeared to be the might of Soviet officialdom. I thought this was extraordinary. I wasn't the leader of this student group and, in normal circumstances, was far from being the noisiest. But all those years of arguments with my Dad, of listening to his stories of negotiation at work, of learning how to look for an angle, had been lessons I had learned particularly well. Like Dad, I didn't appreciate a refusal without a reason, I thought authority should be accountable and, above all, I enjoyed a good game of cat and mouse. You didn't need to make an exhibition of yourself to be effective. And if, in the process, you did draw attention to yourself, this was still respectable because you were trying to do the right thing. 'It's about getting things to your liking, Susan,' he'd always say, with his constant ironic smile.

37

'You think you can walk on water...!'

The unvarnished truth about life in a Soviet student hostel was not something I was ever prepared to commit to paper until I was safely back home. Yet, if I was being very careful in all my correspondence, expecting that the whole lot would be read, and not just by the Russians, my Dad was unexpectedly thorough in his letter-writing. It was a winter of strikes and unrest which saw the entire country working a three-day week and coping with power cuts. By the beginning of 1974 the crisis had forced a general election which led to the fall of the Conservative government under Edward Heath. The entire saga was recounted by my Dad in amused disgust in letters to Moscow. I am sure it had occurred to him that a right to privacy was the most obvious casualty of the Cold War but it clearly didn't bother him. He had loved the trip to Moscow, found it all absolutely fascinating, and was only too happy to offer his impressions and opinions to anyone who cared to ask.

So he enjoyed the on-going connection with things Russian which Sheffield's new town-twinning arrangements provided. The city had formed a link with the Soviet steel city of Donetsk in east Ukraine: as its name suggested, it too was to be found on the banks of the River Don, a name which simply means 'water' in the ancient language of the north Caucasus. I was just back from my year of language study abroad when a 'fraternal delegation' of trade unionists from Donetsk spent a week in Sheffield. A feature entitled 'The Russians in Sheffield', complete with the Soviet hammer and sickle emblem, appeared each night in 'The Star'. Dad delightedly sent me the cuttings from the local paper describing their tour of Firth Brown's Heavy Machine Shop: 'The delegates were fortunate in seeing the tapping of sixty tons of high quality Sheffield steel from a new £3 million electric arc furnace. The Russians listened to Mr Frank Allott, manager of the heavy machine shop, as he told them that his daughter, Susan, a former pupil at Sheffield Girls' High School, had only a fortnight ago returned from Moscow where she has been spending six months studying Russian.'

Though I read the cutting in toe-curling embarrassment there was no mistaking the pride in my Dad's actions. What Russia had done for us both was to help us rebuild the closeness we had lost beside the sea in Yarmouth. Already I was finding it hard to think of the events of that summer without a sinking feeling of remorse for the distress I had caused both my parents. On the surface I remained just as uncompromising as ever but it was already clear that my romantic adventure was not going to end well. Back in the windswept terraced streets of Bradford, Steve and I were far from being the only couple who had been far too young and foolish to deal with a six-month separation. When we finally split up, I took the bus down to Sheffield to break the news. My Mum, as I had hoped, was all solicitude and sympathy. Whatever her feelings at the start of all of this she was always, unfailingly, on my side. My Dad's reaction was one I had not anticipated and whirled me back two years to the beginning of our unexpected estrangement. 'Well,' he said, laying his fork on the edge of his boiled ham salad, 'if you will get yourself into these entanglements....' It was the only time since the ill-fated trip to Yarmouth that he ever let his disappointment and disapproval of my actions show. Yet I had no intention of letting him see how his words had shocked me. 'Look,' I said, resolutely, 'I'd do exactly the same thing all over again. I have no regrets about it at all.' 'Oh,' he said, going back to the lettuce and salad cream. 'Well don't go rushing into anything,' he added, after the awkward pause, attempting to convey something important across the gulf we had created. 'Of course I won't,' I said. But, as usual at that time, I still wasn't listening.

In the event neither of us had time to dwell on any of this. I had a degree to work for and he had Machine Shops to run in a climate at Firth Brown which was getting noticeably trickier. What was more, there were further foreign trips in the offing, and none of them looked like being as pleasant as Canada had been. Nevertheless he began the first of them, to Turkey in 1975, in high enough spirits: 'Just arrived at the Istanbul Hilton which is a most marvellous place. First impressions of the city and Turkey in general very mixed. Iyiyim Allah Isharlardik (Beat that)', the postcard brightly announced. Unfortunately the Hilton was not in charge of the bus which jolted out, hour after hour, along the Black Sea coast to Eregli, nor of the conditions and cuisine on site.

The visit was an enormous struggle. The steelworkers in Turkey lacked the skill and experience of the Canadians. As a result, my Dad found himself personally overseeing the back up roll production process for much of the non-stop forty-eight hours required, whilst the work was interrupted by five daily sets of ablutions and prayers. Always one for holiday stomach upsets he found the food impossible to digest, compounding the exhaustion of the work. He came back with a bagful of beaten copper and carved onyx, star and crescent bracelets for me and Mum, and endless stories of the kindness of the Turkish families who had shown him hospitality in Eregli. But he was very much hoping that the process would not need to be repeated, fearing that it almost certainly would.

The second trip the following year was more gruelling still, with the summer heat to contend with. The postcard that arrived was a masterpiece of understatement: 'Temperature ninety degrees, very pleasant on the terrace overlooking Bosphorus, much warmer in steel mills,' he wrote. The entire business wore him out but, predictably, he never took a day off work on his return. He didn't do that kind of thing. And, anyway, why worry when, somewhere deep inside, you think you're immortal? That's what my Mum was convinced he thought, anyway. Certainly, it was often the way he behaved. Her anxiety at its potential effect on his health would betray itself in rare flashes of exasperation: 'It's no good talking to you,' she would snap suddenly, lip quivering, 'you think you can walk on water!' His response to this would invariably be some quip making light of the matter and an ironic smile which would enrage her so much she would have to walk out of the room. If he wasn't going to take his health seriously, she would just have to to do all the worrying for him.

38

'Driving with Goebbels...'

Away in Bradford, concerned with my studies and professional qualifications, I hadn't really noticed any of this going on. It was only when we went on holiday to Wales together when I had just received my teaching certificate that it became clear to me that something was wrong. My Dad had recently got back from the second trip to Turkey and had decided that a restful stay in the Welsh mountains and a nice bit of touring in his car would be just the thing. I had been thinking that I really needed to learn to drive now that I would be working as a teacher and he, ever helpful to my ambitions, had immediately offered to teach me. It was a classic example of mutual amnesia, as if all my uncoordinated childhood years in shorts had been completely erased from both our minds. Not to mention the fact that it was a lunatic way to spend a holiday for someone who was in need of a rest.

My Dad loved his car. Not that he ever went very far in it. In an average ten years, once he stopped driving between the Firth Derihon factories, he would never do more than 30,000 miles. But he took a pleasure in driving that no doubt had a lot to do with coming to it so late. And when driving was something he was so naturally talented at he had simply assumed that I would be too. But, as I should have realised, great skills don't always make great teachers. My first mistake was letting him choose the spot to start. In the Welsh mountains, finding an appropriate piece of road for a beginner was no simple matter. Our first lesson took place halfway down a mountain road on a very short side track leading to a five-barred gate and woodland plunging into a brook below. There was just enough space to 'release the clutch, press the accelerator, release the handbrake', drive for three feet and then slam on the brake. My Dad seemed surprised that this introduction to 'starting the vehicle' had not increased my confidence. Still, the gate remained intact and there were only a couple of flakes off the paint on the bonnet so this was adjudged a reasonable success.

The second lesson took place on a single-track one-in-six mountain road with a wall of shale on one side and a grassy descent to the river on the other. My task was to set off (as previously taught) and proceed downhill into second gear before applying the brakes at the ninety-degree bend a hundred yards ahead. On completion of this manoevre, Dad would turn the car around on the wide bit of the bend and back we would go to the top. It must have been somewhere around this time that he noticed I had started shaking. I can remember him looking at me, genuinely mystified, clearly thinking that, if he'd been in the driving seat, we would have been in Bangor by now.

The third and final lesson began with a search for a flat piece of road. There weren't any. But there was a caravan park just across the river with a sign saying 'Strictly Private'. I was amazed to watch my fanatically law-abiding father drive boldly through the gates and walk round to the passenger's side. I was just beginning to think that third gear might be the one for me after all when the proprietor emerged from a luxury mobile home at the far end of the field. 'What exactly are you doing?!' she demanded. 'I'm just giving my daughter here a driving lesson,' Dad replied calmly and with breathtaking cheek as we were ordered off the site. My only contribution to this exchange was an embarrassed grimace. It was dawning on me that the man who ran Firth Brown's machine shops was perhaps not quite the same as the model citizen who turned up at home.

It was, nevertheless, the defining moment in a mutually-agreed cessation of tuition. It was a great relief to both of us. By now it was clear to me that it was not merely my lack of driving skill that was pushing up his blood pressure. I spent the rest of the week teaching him some relaxation techniques. At least that was something I could do successfully. Satisfyingly, we were both able to blame the abandonment of the driving lessons on the thoughtlessness of the Welsh landscape, rather than any mutual shortcomings. We both knew, of course, that 'driving with Goebbels', as I later came to call it, was at the bottom of my subsequent failure to pass a driving test until I was thirty-four. 'Lucky you had all those good lessons with me to start you off!' he said, ruefully, when I finally threw away the L-plates.

39

'I don't want some idiot making decisions on my behalf...'

Back at Firth Brown the climate had been steadily changing. It began in the early seventies with rumours of mergers and takeovers. When Oliver Jessel finally bought the firm his reputation as an asset stripper went before him. The disquiet which this development engendered deepened in the light of the recession which followed the 1974 oil crisis. As world demand for steel slumped and competition with foreign producers became more intense the impact of years of under-investment began to make itself felt. Firth Brown's directors had scarcely been alone in a tendency to cream off the profits, to plough their massive liquidity into investments in all directions except on the shop floor. When customers were literally queueing up for steel it might appear churlish to accuse them of a lack of vision. Yet, from his vantage point in the research laboratories, Derek Taylor had felt some concern many years earlier: 'They were so successful and so wealthy that they just didn't see that there would ever be any serious competition. Our research lads would go out to places like India and Thailand and teach them how to make the steel. It'd be clog iron, basically. We used to call it clog iron. And what happened of course was predictable. We went out there teaching them and the next thing you know they're making it cheaper and we couldn't compete.'

As far as investment was concerned there was an element of caution which, from the directors' perspective, could look like simple common sense. When steel had become a political football with constant talk of nationalisation, denationalisation or renationalisation from the end of the Second World War until

1967 there was an undoubted logic to hanging on to the cash. By the time Jessel arrived on the scene the economic situation was already looking more threatening, as his new employees were well aware. I remember the looks which passed between people and the comments that were quietly made one summer Saturday as he spun into sight in his helicopter over Firth Brown's sports field. Although, as he glad-handed the sports day's dignitaries at one end of the field, my attention was distracted by the sight of my Dad winning the Veterans' Race. He had not long retired from refereeing professionally and was made to start at least sixty yards behind the other contestants. The wiry figure with the slightly bow legs duly sauntered past everyone else on the final bend to general acclaim, leaving Jessel forgotten by me at any rate.

In the event, the results of the Jessel purchase were unexpected. Far from subjecting the firm to a cut and run campaign he described Firth Brown as 'the jewel in my crown' - that phrase again - and began to use the capital from investments to re-equip. By all previous standards it was big money - a million or more in every machine shop or department. Outside of the fire-struck Heavy Machine Shop most of the machine tools had been in place since the 1920s and the managers with new money in their pockets now had the opportunity to see at first hand exactly what they were up against in Italy and Germany. Even this spending spree would not be enough to get ahead of the competition though it would do something to arrest the decline.

Amongst the managers the arrival of Oliver Jessel finally spurred them to do something which had been discussed for some time, namely to organise themselves into a branch of a trade union. At a specially-convened meeting of all the managers my Dad was formally elected Chair, with Derek Taylor as Secretary, of the Executive Branch of ASTMS. As Derek said, there was much talk on the lines of 'you know how to talk to them, we've got total confidence in you' but, when push came to shove, 'no-one else was actually willing to put their heads above the parapet.' Besides which, as both Derek and my Dad agreed, you never knew what turn events might take. 'I had every intention of being in control of this,' my Dad had characteristically said at the time, 'I don't want some idiot making decisions on my behalf that I'm supposed to stick to.'

They must have made an interesting team, Derek and my Dad; Derek with his forthright and impetuous nature and his uncompromising politics, wanting to 'get up and at 'em', as he put it, my Dad with his caution and his quiet deviousness, always enjoying the cunning way around a problem. There were, inevitably, some differences of opinion but they were readily resolved, as Derek later described:

'Frank and I had developed rather a civilised habit of my being invited, or inviting myself, to urgent "conferences" in Frank's office which was nicely tucked away in a remote corner of the plant where few directors had the inclination, or courage, to tread. His office was rather on the small side but was nicely protected on both entrance points by a short corridor and two outer offices. Here sat his henchmen who would die rather than admit anyone into the inner sanctum at these important times. Despite these two drawbridges being raised, when I went into his office he would carefully lock the door. Then he would reach in his desk for a key to his furthest filing cabinet to extract a bottle of Bells whisky and two drinking vessels, the shape and colour and apparent texture of miniature beer barrels. As far as I remember, Frank, as was his general nature, was somewhat more disciplined than me and restricted himself to a maximum of two tots. I, I'm sad to say, particularly since I can't recall actually buying a bottle of whisky for these sessions, frequently extended it to three and, in moments requiring considerable stress relief, even four. Frank tended to disapprove of that but, as always, he was the perfect host. These delightful sessions, sometimes running on to six o' clock-ish or so, were not confined to Union business by any means. Our joint interests were catholic. There was hardly anything we couldn't debate, and in its truest sense too. Frank was deeper than I was. I never debated in a flippant nature, or on a flippant basis, but my thoughts, frequently, were not nearly so deep as Frank's.'

My Dad enjoyed running ASTMS, he liked the cut and thrust, the problem-solving, the dealing with people. What he couldn't stand were meetings for the sake of meetings or people who loved to hear the sound of their own voice, whether or not they actually had anything to say. 'People just can't keep on the subject,' he would complain to me. 'If you give some people half a chance they're off all over the place.' He had, he said, discovered the perfect way to call them to a halt. 'I don't know,' he'd say from the Chair, 'you'll be telling us about your grandmother's bad knee next!'

'I know what it was you were drinking out of, Derek,' I said, years later, on the day he and I met up to talk about Firth Brown after my Dad's death. We sat back in our chairs after lunch, surrounded by his local pub's Christmas decorations whilst the familiar Christmas songs played on, 'They were part of a set. They must have been a present when I was very small. There was a pottery decanter in the shape of a Dutch boy holding a bottle. You took the cap off the bottle and that was the spout and then there were six of these little pottery barrels you arranged around him for glasses. He must have taken them to work. My mother's still got them on the shelf.' 'Has she really?' he exclaimed, 'Oh, I'd love one of them. We had some happy times, what you might call old stagers or something. We had our moments.' I sent him one of the barrels after Christmas, packed and padded into a Jiffy bag with a miniature bottle of Bells. It felt nice to send it. But it felt strange to think of him drinking it on his own.

40

'I wouldn't be like that...'

If ASTMS, by and large, was a pleasure the same could not be said of the job as a whole any more. And it wasn't the advent of Oliver Jessel that caused all the trouble; it had begun with a change of personnel rather closer to home. Quite suddenly, and with an immense shock to my Dad, Ken Bliss died. In all the years since my father had come from Firth Derihon, Ken had been the manager of the Light Machine Shop. Their oddly parallel careers had placed them, in the end, in exactly equivalent positions. But, as times had got tougher, my Dad had seen less and less of his old friend. Ken had started to decline invitations to go out for a glass of beer, citing pressure of work. On the occasions when they did manage to meet up, my Dad would come back looking concerned, telling us that Ken had talked obsessively about the firm all night. Dad had tried taking him to play snooker to get him to relax but, even then, he'd reported, 'He just can't talk about anything else. He can't leave it alone at all. I don't think that does you any good.' He was worried about the amount of work Ken was taking home with him, the constant anxiety that was going home with it. And then, out of the blue, Ken was taken ill. And then he was dead. And all the warnings had come to nothing.

'I wouldn't be like that. I wouldn't do what Ken did,' my Dad, in the stunned aftermath, was at pains to reassure us. And it was true, he didn't bring home piles of work or talk obsessively about the job all the time. But he did often sit, withdrawn into silence, utterly preoccupied by a problem at work. He did take the phone calls in the evenings and at weekends from anxious foremen when jobs were going wrong. He did rush down there at odd hours, late at night, in attempts to limit damage, pulling on his coat, shouting '30,000 quid this job's worth!' as he raced to the car. He did wake long before dawn, turning on the light to write down an idea he'd had in the notebook he kept constantly at his bedside, lying awake until the alarm clock would let him get stuck in again. Even from a distance the deterioration was obvious, even without my Mum discreetly informing on him in telephone calls when he wasn't around. There began to be talk of blood pressure problems.

It was his feet that saved him, Mum and I always thought. Years of cutting V-shapes into the centre of his big toe nails had failed, ultimately, to prevent the increasingly incapacitating pain. Ingrowing toenails, like wisdom teeth, are one of those things which sound trivial but are utterly excruciating. They were such a mess in the end that the tops of his toes were going to have to come off. My Dad presented himself at the Infirmary and, once on the ward, asked if he could pay for a private room. The doctor wanted to know why. He explained about his job and how he'd been feeling in the months before the feet had, literally, brought him to a standstill. He was promptly given a private room for free, a gesture which pleased him a great deal but probably ought to have worried him a lot more. It was whilst he was recovering from the operation that a curious incident took place which characterised the shift in attitudes at Firth Brown.

During the seventies, Firth Brown had taken over the Glasgow firm of Beardmores. It had been a huge Scottish institution, employing 50-60,000 men at one time. They had made aircraft, ships, armaments and ordnance, but the firm had dwindled away to become a shell of its former self. By the 1970s they were predominantly a maker of rolls and this was the business which interested Firth Brown. When it was first taken over it was managed from Sheffield – 'a most remarkable affair,' as Derek Taylor put it, 'something else Frank used to do in his spare time!' Several of the Firth Brown managers of the day would regularly go up to Beardmores to oversee the running of the place. I recall my

Dad describing his first naive attempt to go for a quiet drink in a Glasgow city centre pub after work and being carefully escorted by the landlord into a private lounge bar for his own safety. In due course the management issues were sorted out, both in Glasgow and Sheffield, with the result that Sheffield acquired a new Works Director drafted in from Beardmores.

As my Dad was recovering, shortly after his operation, the Works Director suddenly came marching into the ward outside visiting hours, demanding answers to a problem. It was an event which upset and disturbed my Dad, bothered as he was in any case by the pressure of the job. The entire point of having a private room was negated at a stroke. My mother was absolutely beside herself. All the anxiety and distress came pouring out until the man's name could scarcely be breathed in her presence. In days to come my Dad insisted on lightening things a bit by making a joke of her response. 'Your mother doesn't like him and she's never even met him,' he'd say. 'How can you be like that? I think she's being completely unreasonable to the poor man!' 'Poor man!' she'd exclaim and stomp off, spitting feathers. But my Dad was more than a little dismayed at the ruthlessness he'd witnessed. Lying in pyjamas in a hospital bed is not, after all, the ideal way to fight one's corner. It didn't bode well for the new regime.

It got worse by the the time my Dad's final foreign trip was on the agenda in 1978. It was Brazil, with an exhausting transatlantic flight and a tough schedule to follow it. On arrival things didn't seem so bad as he still had the energy left to be astonished by Rio de Janeiro, both its extraordinary setting and its dire poverty: 'beautiful but dangerous', was how he summed it up. It would probably have been fine if the steel mills had been on Copacabana Avenue next to the hotel where they had unexpectedly provided him with a suite. Instead he embarked on a series of visits to Sao Paolo and Brasilia then flew into the interior in a small plane to the head office of Usiminas at Belo Horizonte. From there he flew to the steel mills at Ipatinga, a large modern city in the Rio Doce valley which had been a tiny village a mere twenty years earlier. Designed by the architect of Brasilia, this was a place which could ignore the industry which sustained it as the dense Brazilian forest divided the city centre from the steel works.

The processing of the rolls was carried out in searing heat. It was November and summer had just hit Brazil with a vengeance. Worst of all, the stomach problems which had made a misery of my Dad's trips to Turkey caused him trouble once again. He returned on a Monday, completely exhausted, utterly jet-lagged, cramped with violent diarrhoea. Ignoring my mother's entreaties, he was back in the Machine Shop on Tuesday morning. By the end of the 1970s running the Heavy Machine Shops had become one long worry; he was convinced he couldn't afford to leave it even one more day. If the implications terrified my Mum, for my Dad it was simply another triumph of mind over matter. Unforunately, by this stage, he had been pushing his luck a bit too long. Three months later he was in intensive care.

41

'The winter of discontent...'

My Dad arrived back in Sheffield at the height of what came to be known as 'the winter of discontent'. It was 1979 and just about everybody seemed to be on strike. Where things were still moving the weather produced its own paralysis. It snowed heavily and went on snowing. Getting to work seemed arduous and difficult, even in a city where the bus routes were kept clear. In Sheffield the council workers responsible for snow clearance decided to go on strike. It was a hard winter. My Grandma was taken ill in what proved to be the beginning of her final illness. My Mum, caring for her and worrying about my Dad since his return from Brazil, was being sent off to the hospital with disturbing symptoms of her own. But he was still doing his job, concerned to see that his visit to Brazil had a successful outcome. 'Dear Friend Elisio', he wrote privately from his home address to his colleague in Ipatinga, explaining that the Back-up Roll Sleeves were awaiting shipment. Clearly hoping to ensure that the men in Brazil would be able to cope without his supervision, he added a drawing and his own comments and explanations of what Elisio would receive, with an invitation to contact him directly at any time if something was unclear. 'I often think of you in Brazil as we are having a very hard winter. For a number of weeks now we have had snow and temperatures of minus ten to minus fourteen. It is the worst winter for more than twenty years, I shall have to come and see you to get warm.'

Snow, darkness, fatigue and illness, with an ill-defined anxiety that worse was to come, seemed to be the only themes the length of this pitiless February. As the snow piled up in the Sheffield streets my Dad began abandoning his car when driving further became impossible, walking home in the bitter wind, his scarf pulled up around his mouth and nose. Listening to local radio to check on the progress of the strike negotiations my mother was beside herself to hear the leader of the council 'gritters' say that they would not call off their action. 'It looks as if there'll be more snow,' he had said, an unmistakeably smug note in his voice. Not long after, the ambulance men came out on strike too. For my Mum the ever-present anxiety was beginning to turn to fear. Unavoidably, there were now a lot more desperate evenings when my Dad trudged miles through the snow and ice, and freezing mornings when he set off early to attempt to rescue his car.

One night at the end of February he couldn't sleep. There were severe pains in his arm and chest. Sweat was pouring off him. There was also, as he admitted later, the long dark tunnel and the clear bright light. He wouldn't let my Mum call the doctor. He waited until the morning, decided he was cured and was about to set off for work until she persuaded him to make for the local surgery instead. The doctor listened to his story and calmly told him to drive back home and get back into bed. He would contact the hospital. It was six hours before the ambulance arrived to deposit him in intensive care where the sudden flurry of testing and monitoring made it clear that something was badly wrong. He had had a major heart attack which, as he later discovered, had caused massive and irreparable damage to his heart. He was incredibly lucky to be alive.

Characteristically, in a couple of days he was back on the ward, laughing and joking and generally entertaining his visitors. He was completely unable to take in what had happened to him. To the day he was discharged, slowly gathering his belongings and walking down the ward, he was still waiting. It was only a matter of time, he was sure, until a fresh-faced young doctor would come rushing towards him, papers in hand: 'we're terribly sorry, Mr. Allott, we've made a dreadful mistake. We got your test results mixed up with somebody else's. It wasn't a heart attack at all.' It was only when they let him finally walk out of the ward that he realised they were never coming to tell him. He was stuck with it. He was always a lousy patient, even if it was only a spot of flu. The heart attack knocked the wind out of his sails, depressing him with the discovery that even he couldn't walk on water indefinitely. 'I feel useless,' he kept saying, miserably. There was nothing more damning than that in his entire vocabulary. But things could get worse. A couple of weeks later two of his foremen came to see him to tell him about developments at work.

With my Dad temporarily off the scene the Works Director had moved swiftly. Ken Bliss's successor as manager of the Light Machine Shops was promptly placed in charge of both the Light and Heavy Machine Shops. My Dad was neither consulted nor even directly informed. The first he heard of this aid to convalescence was when the foremen turned up at home with the news. It came as a bombshell. After all, no-one had suggested that he would be unable to resume his job in due course. Worse than that, he would now be returning to an entirely different situation.

From a position of total authority over the affairs of the Heavy Machine Shops he was suddenly answerable to someone else. It would not, perhaps, have been so bad if that someone else had been of equivalent knowledge and experience. But his new boss had never been in charge of anything of the complexity of the Heavy Machine Shops: in the view of my Dad and his friends in management, he would scarcely be in a position to offer leadership to someone who had been running the place for a decade. There was no chance now of a steady convalescence, of 'at least six weeks off and a month on half-days,' as the doctors had prescribed. Within a month my Dad was back at Firth Brown working half-time. Yet, as soon as he saw the realities of the situation which now confronted him, he realised that he could not afford to betray any weakness. Within two days he was working full time, business as usual. Except that there was no 'as usual' any more.

However appalled he was at the loss of his autonomy he had no choice now but to refer all his decisions to his new superior. 'It's absolutely invidious,' he would say, 'you take a decision which is common sense, no question of whether it's right or wrong, it's the obvious thing to do, and suddenly you've got to answer to somebody who knows nothing about it.' But, just like the heart disease itself, he was stuck with it; a fact his superiors were not slow to point out. As Derek Taylor observed, 'it's actually just insulting when you have all those years of knowledge and experience, and it's even more insulting when the other person knows less. Naturally, you would be incensed about that. And I can imagine it might have had a significant effect on Frank's health.' Certainly, it would be difficult to think of anything less calculated to soothe the angina which had begun to plague him than the state of subdued rage in which he spent much of his final years at the firm. You couldn't talk to him about it. He would just clench his teeth and look away if ever the subject came up. He left it to my mother to fill in the gaps. The way she expressed it left me in no doubt about how bitter and upset it made him feel.

42

'Restructuring is the new "in" word...'

It was not until some eighteen months after the heart attack that I received the first hint from my Dad that rather more than his health was going badly wrong. I was back in the USSR once more, on a British Council studentship, working for my PhD and we were in regular correspondence, just as we had been during my previous stay seven years before. By now he had doubtless realised that both the women in his life were perpetually anxious about the state of his heart, so his letters were relentlessly upbeat. There were jolly tales of disastrous sequence dancing classes - 'dancing with your mother is like dancing with a reluctant table!' he ungallantly observed. And there were amusing descriptions of his attempts at home brewing which produced a beer mockingly named after their street : 'Chateau Glentilt - puts hairs on your teeth!'

But the first time the situation at Firth Brown was described, in a letter lingeringly handled by the minders at the doors of my hostel in Minsk, there was no disguising the seriousness of the situation. My Dad's agitation leapt off the page in a piece entirely lacking in full stops: 'I am adding a few lines as I am not at work today, the whole of Firth Browns are on a four-day week until further notice, certainly until the end of the year, there is not really a financial problem for people, as we are paid through Government seventy-five per cent of our normal earnings, called Temporary Short Time Working subsidy, but I deplore the reasons for it, which are entirely to do with the Government's high interest rates, which means that firms are borrowing money at a higher rate than they can earn profits.'

In the wake of the 'winter of discontent' we had a new government, led by Margaret Thatcher, with a deeply ideological commitment to monetarist economic policies directed primarily at the control of inflation. What this would mean in practice for British manufacturing was beginning to become all too clear. But the situation at Firth Brown was complicated by a range of underlying factors which made the firm particularly vulnerable to the Thatcherite economic experiment.

From the outside, it was by no means apparent that there was any weakness in the company. There had, after all, been a major investment programme through the 1970s. There was the state-of-the-art electric arc furnace which the Russian visitors had been so proudly shown in 1973. In addition, my Dad had been sent to Austria, Belgium and Italy to look at prospective purchases during this process of re-equipment. He had negotiated the purchase of a gigantic GSM from Linz – 'the biggest cheque I ever signed in my life', as one of Firth Brown's former directors later described it to me. 'They were queuing up for steel,' the director remarked – by no means the only person to use exactly these words – 'so it was a very short time indeed until the total collapse.' In 1978, Princess Margaret had paid an official visit to the firm, my Dad telling us of his surprise both at how petite she was and how enormous was the jewel which glittered on her finger. As he guided her around the Machine Shops there was plenty to show off for the admiration of royalty.

The problem for Firth Brown, as the major company left outside the nationalised steel industry, was that uncomfortable competition was not merely coming from abroad. The presence of BSC (the British Steel Corporation), and the terms on which this state-owned company operated, consistently distorted the market. It was a point which I recall my Dad continually and exasperatedly making whenever the steel industry was discussed on TV or in the papers. As Derek Taylor summarised it: 'BSC was cushioned by the government, choose what they did they were subsidised. They weren't allowed to make a loss, but if they did it was absorbed, and their salaries were at least twenty-five or thirty percent greater than ours. But the point is, they maintained those salaries, they didn't have to make a profit to exist, but we did to survive as a private company. You had to make a profit and if you didn't the company collapsed. So we faced competition from BSC, who competed for the same business as us but were cushioned by the government, also the Third World countries, so the whole thing accelerated quite considerably. So it was not simple.' It was, effectively, a kind of pincer movement, gradually strangling the private companies: 'There was no doubt of that,' Derek said, 'and we were very bitter about that. We met on joint committees and we weren't slow to make that point, and we would make it vociferously.'

Now, at the beginning of the 1980s, a new government was in power which had already made it clear that there would be no more expensive bailouts on the lines of the deal through which a previous government had saved Rolls Royce. For Margaret Thatcher's Conservative government the market was king, and the market would be the arbiter. Any who could not compete would go to the wall. It was, they insisted, a fundamental law of capitalism. The only problem was that no such 'fundamental law' actually existed in its pure form. There were rules, both at UK and European Community level, and there were levers. There were also ideologies and bad memories. This was a government whose Conservative predecessor under Edward Heath had been utterly humiliated by the trade unions in the early seventies. Our new Prime Minister had formed part of that government and had clearly not forgotten the bitter lessons she had learned. Moreover, her government had come to power on a wave of public and media disapproval of the havoc created by industrial action in the winter of 1979. They were in no mood to listen to any special pleadings from industry. As Derek commented, 'Well, we all know what Thatcher was like, I mean I can't describe her politely. But she was already having to subsidise a company, BSC, that she didn't want nationalised anyway. So she certainly wasn't going to lift a finger to help those in the private sector. They had to look after themselves.'

More to the point, it began to become clear that this was a government which was not simply antagonistic to the trade unions but had little sympathy for, or understanding of, the UK's traditional industries. A new European Community agreement aimed at reducing supply in the European steel industry was insisting both on plant closures and an end to government subsidies; it could scarcely have been more in tune with the UK government's ideological stance. As other European partners took action in the face of this central directive to protect their national steel industries, the UK zealously set about fulfilling the European proposals.

At the same time, the new regime in Westminster began to tackle inflation, their major priority, through a range of policies which rapidly led to soaring interest rates and a strong pound. The results for the whole of UK industry were immediate and deeply worrying: loans on which industry relied for investment became prohibitively expensive and the strength of the UK currency made our exports far more expensive for foreign buyers. By the autumn of 1980, as orders slumped, the impact of these new government policies on manufacturing industry was dramatic enough to lead both the CBI (the Confederation of British Industry) and over 300 leading economists to call for an immediate abandonment of the experiment.

For the steel industry, the sudden severe depression which hit the UK economy brought about a drastic decline in domestic demand. At the same time, demand from abroad fell as the exchange rate made its exports too expensive for foreign buyers. Orders were lost by firms which were simultaneously struggling to meet the entirely unexpected costs arising from crippling interest rates. It was, literally, a lethal cocktail. All pleas to the government to change course fell on deaf ears. Instead, we were constantly treated to lectures about British industry's lack of competitiveness and the need to become 'leaner and fitter'. But, as I knew from the horse's mouth, in my Dad's machine shops there had been no lack of export orders; if we had suddenly become uncompetitive, it had come about by deliberate government policy, from politicians who were determined to teach the workers a lesson. Flying in the face of all the economic evidence, the Thatcher government was adamant that there was no alternative.

When my Dad's first mention of the local fallout from all of this appeared in his letter to Minsk my reaction had been alarmed and, probably, too unguarded. Over subsequent months his letters were careful to make scant reference to his concerns. He doubtless thought, quite rightly as it turned out, that I had enough to worry about, coping with life in the USSR on my own. Yet there was still quite enough in the letters to make the seriousness of the situation crystal clear:

'Restructuring is now taking place at Firth Browns, that is the new "in" word for chopping off activities that are not too profitable and making people redundant. There were ninety-five told last Friday that they were to finish and I feel that there will be many more.'

'We have now only four weeks to work until we finish for Christmas. This year the holiday will be longer than ever because of the shortage of work, ie. from the 19th December until 5th January.'

'BSC are going to stop at least 20,000.'

'The Labour Party is, as usual, in complete disarray, and this at a time of the most incompetent and reactionary Conservative government in living memory.'

By the time I got back home for the first-hand story the storm clouds had well and truly settled overhead.

In dealing with the day to day effects of the crises which unfolded through the collapse of steel in the early eighties my Dad felt that his hands were absolutely tied by his superiors in the firm. The management reorganisation which had followed his heart attack meant that he was simply no longer his own man. By the time Firth Brown and the BSC River Don Works were shrinking into the new Sheffield Forgemasters, he had had enough. They were not offering him a redundancy package, quite the reverse. He was offered a senior position in the new company; doubtless they still needed his skills. But, finally, at the age of fifty-eight, he no longer needed them. He took a good look at the state of his pension fund and handed in his resignation. The men in the 3/4 Machine Shops gave him a fine set of bowls in a leather case as a retirement present. Better still, they made him a replica of the famous back up roll which had taken him on his travels: even in miniature its weight jerked down the wrist of anyone casually picking it up. That weekend we all sat out in the warm summer darkness, watching the champagne cork fly across the grass, assuring him that forty-four years of service was still 'not bad, was it?' An era was ending, in every sense: there was sadness and bewilderment and relief as much as celebration in the bubbles.

43

'Them jobs'll never return...'

Where did the steelworks go? It was almost as if one day they were there, vast and unmissable as always, the next they were gone. And the land where they had stood was transformed almost overnight in a devastation so complete it resembled not so much Dresden as Hiroshima. From the city centre's eastern edges to the soaring motorway at Tinsley, mile upon mile of scorched earth bore nothing but the outlines of machine shop foundations. These living and working memorials to the Industrial Revolution had become as distant, suddenly, as the Roman Empire, as unimaginable from their traces as Hadrian's Wall. Going down to stare at the immensity of this nothingness required a stronger stomach than I possessed: I only went down there once, in the summer of 1985, after I had heard what was happening, driving down to Sheffield especially to see the steelworks one last time. I was already too late. The loss of landmarks disorientated me, the roads were already leading nowhere. When I got out of the car to photograph familiar walls, gaping and roofless already in mid-demolition, I found myself hurrying, fumbling awkwardly with the shutter, feeling like someone who had gatecrashed a funeral.

I made it worse, of course, by going back to Petre Street. Standing on a grassy hillside where the rows and rows of brick terraces had been, overlooking the blankness of the Don Valley, I was joined by an elderly chap in an old khaki mac and flat cap who had just toiled up the hill. 'You look like somebody who's lost something,' he said, smiling ruefully, clearly knowing exactly what it was. We stood together on the end of Petre Street, imagining the bus shelter and the sweet shop, the Co-op dry cleaners and the chip shop, Sutherland Road Baths and the old massive spire of All Saints church. I told him how we had lived in the shadow of the steeple and how I had gone round there with my parents when they had begun the demolition. 'You can't go in there when they're demolishing it!' my Mum had exclaimed with her customary caution. 'Yes, we can,' my Dad had replied, leading the way past the 'Danger. Keep Out' signs to tour the vanished church where they had been married. 'Come on,' he said, 'let's walk down the aisle again!' He took her by the arm and they strode between imaginary pews, humming Mendelssohn, down to the yawning hole at the foot of the towering steeple, standing now in glorious isolation. The old man laughed at the story and turned to wave his hand across the sweep of the valley, 'but it's this that's the tragedy. It's an absolute tragedy. It'll never come back now. Them jobs'll never return.'

I never went back again to survey the final triumph of the demolition gangs. It was bad enough seeing it from the train. Even from within the air-conditioned capsule of an InterCity you could feel the eeriness of the place, half-expecting survivors to stumble towards you, wide-eyed and uncomprehending, from the midst of the rubble. Only in Westminster could you imagine this was industry becoming 'leaner and fitter'. From the vantage point of the Don Valley, it looked very different. It was a de-industrialisation, a cultural revolution, Chairman Mao would have been proud of.

If the look of it shocked and frightened people, the reality of redundancies, early retirements and long-term unemployment cut far deeper. For those, like my Dad, who had indifferent health and years of contributions to a decent pension fund, the collapse of steel might prove a personal blessing. In the normal course of events he would have soldiered on to retirement age and might well have been defeated in the attempt by the heart disease. The massive shake-up of closures and mergers made him realise he was in no state to spearhead an entirely new venture at Forgemasters, the future which was being suggested to him. To the great relief of us all he began what he called in the end 'the best fifteen years of my life'. Yet even for the lucky few in such a position as this there was no escaping the impact of the change. It was everywhere: in the loss of apprenticeships and openings for the young, in the lack of security for the middle-aged, in the tens of thousands who were forced to leave the city in search of work elsewhere, in the dismay and disorientation which seemed to descend upon Sheffield as a whole. A week never seemed to go by without further evidence of devastation emerging in phone calls or visits home.

My Dad, in particular, took it very hard. The sweeping away of the steelworks seemed like a personal affront, an assault on his identity as someone who had worked a lifetime there, an attack on his notions of dignity and of the value of skilled craftsmanship. He was appalled at the idea that highly skilled work requiring a seven-year apprenticeship could be just as well replaced by any old jobs in retailing or service industries, just as long as they made up the numbers. He was utterly disgusted at politicians' apparent satisfaction in creating what he called 'Mickey Mouse' jobs in fast food outlets and tourist venues, and wondered how making a fast buck had suddenly become the acme of morality. 'It's come to something when a Tory government won't even listen to the CBI. They'll not be right until they've destroyed this country,' he used to say. By the mid-1980s the Conservatives had decisively avenged their humiliation at the hands of the unions and produced the compliant workforce they had so desired. But my Dad was convinced that the long-term cost of this would prove to be far greater than anyone suspected.

'Who's making the wealth for this country now?' he would regularly demand, committing to memory import and export figures which he would produce at the drop of a hat whenever anyone began to argue that the Thatcher government had done the country a service. Throughout his retirement, against a backdrop of media triumphalism about Britain's apparently booming economy, he never stopped asking the same question: how was it possible that financial services and property speculation could replace manufacturing exports as the backbone of the economy? 'It's a bubble, Susan,' he would say, presciently as it turned out, 'and we're all going to regret it in years to come.' In the end, it was this and not the emotional attachment to Sheffield steel, which was the nub of the matter as far as he was concerned. The monetarist ideologues of the Thatcher years stood condemned, in his eyes, not for their demolition of jobs or unions, but for their utter lack of patriotism. 'The Germans have still got a steel industry,' he would say, shaking his head, 'they managed not to be so stupid.'

44

'All this knowledge not being used...'

In the summer of 1983, as the demolition gangs spread out across Sheffield's east end, my Dad packed away all of his notebooks, manuals and calculations into his big black briefcase and stowed them away in a corner of the spare bedroom. That, he assumed, was that. But during the next year he was contacted, to his surprise, by Firth Vickers who were having problems with a series of jobs for Rolls Royce. They asked if he might be available to help them. Working on an hourly basis, typically undercharging them, he could at least go in and out at his discretion, overseeing operations, producing endless columns of figures and pages of notes, minute by minute breakdowns of machining. Jobs were detailed meticulously through the day, from '9.43 Set tools' to '14.55 File corners. Complete' and with each job an exact account was attached of the time he had spent to receive his hourly rate: '5 hours 12 minutes, less 53 minutes lunch, total 4 hours 19 minutes.' All this was followed by a detailed analysis of the machining and descriptions of the problems encountered: 'Bore not cleaning up. Tip failed after 2" deeper cut to clean. ... Tip shattered when breaking through. Toolholder base damaged, touched up on shop grinder. Refitted. ... Many problems on cutting bore. Operator went to hospital with cut finger. No further trials on this one.'

As always, there was his overriding concern with efficiency and speed of working: 'Consider 15 minutes wasted in last 30 minutes in an effort to lengthen time. ... Took 11 minutes to set tool. ... To get to this stage, took 24 minutes longer than first one. Try again!!' Alongside his own notes he kept the pages of discussion and specifications of the 'Guide to Sintered Carbides for Machining' from 'Metalworking Production' magazine and a guide to cutting speed and carbide tip grade for alloy steel forgings, treated alloy steel and stainless steel, for immediate reference.

They were extremely pleased with his advice and innovations. 'I am sure that we would not have progressed so quickly without your assistance. Your obvious knowledge of the job and personal integrity assured a high degree of acceptance of new ideas both by Management and operators,' they wrote to him later. But he made it very clear that he was not interested in the job they wanted to offer him. He was getting to like his freedom. They were left with wishing him well in resuming his retirement and hoping he might advise them in the future, 'on a consultancy basis of course'.

It bothered him, none the less, that his skills were going to waste. He used to show me his notebooks, page after page of machine tool speeds and depth of cut calculations. 'Nobody else'll have got anything like this,' he'd say. 'All this knowledge not being used.' It obviously preyed on his mind; just how much came home to me in a conversation we had some five years after his retirement. Having finally gained the academic post I had been working towards for so long, teaching Russian language, I had just come back from a work trip to Moscow. It was 1988 and what came to be known as the 'Moscow Spring' was at its height. My Dad was fascinated by the changes and unprecedented liberal reforms taking place under the new Soviet leader, Mikhail Gorbachev, and had been following events closely on TV and in the press. Most of all he was delighted and relieved at the disarmament negotiations and official visits taking place, the relaxation of tension and the hope that perhaps now, at last, the Cold War could be brought to an end. He wanted to hear about everything I had seen and be the first to know the conclusions I had drawn.

We talked about it all for hours and my Dad, as always, contributed highly perceptive comments and questions to the discussion. But it was the following day before I discovered what was really on his mind. 'I've been thinking,' he said, 'I wonder if they could make use of all this stuff I've got in Russia? You know, I always think, when you see films of Russian steelworks on TV, you can see why they're inefficient because the machines aren't going fast enough. It's dead obvious when you know what they should look like. We ought to go, you and me, we could put 'em straight! It would be nice to do something useful with it all.'

I was amazed, looking at him, to realise that he was entirely serious. He genuinely thought he could turn things around and really wanted to give it a try. He was convinced that now was the time to bury the Cold War hatchet and for all countries to begin to work in partnership across Europe. He thought he could be part of a new people's diplomacy for the peace he had always believed in. To my astonishment, I realised that he could see us as a team, working together, he with the technical know-how, me as interpreter and troubleshooter. Given what I knew of the USSR, however, there could be only one reaction. I could imagine him going crazy at the appalling Soviet working practices, driven wild by the bureaucracy, hating the food. I could imagine my Mum, frantic with worry on her own in Sheffield, struggling with the miseries of East-West phone calls. Most of all, I could see in front of me a man who needed a heart bypass operation. I gently put him off the idea and he rarely mentioned it after that, but I was touched more than I could say that, if he couldn't do much about Sheffield any more, he still wanted to change the world.

45

'With a little help from my friends...'

As for me, it was almost ten years before I set foot in the east end again. I used to drive down from West Yorkshire on the scenic route, avoiding the motorway and the stark changes on the sites where the works had been. Sheffield Arena, Don Valley Stadium, Meadowhall only existed on television, as far as I was concerned. It was unavoidable knowing about it; I just didn't want to look. Like any ex-pat, I had encased my former home in mental bubble-wrap, refusing to encounter its changes in case it was not my city any more. Then, in the early 1990s, my Mum and Dad had moved up to Keighley, to a new house five minutes up the road from me. Always very aware that he was 'living on borrowed time', as he sometimes said after the heart attack, he had jumped at the chance of ensuring my Mum would always be looked after. Once they had moved there were few reasons to go back to Sheffield again.

It was an unlikely thing that made me go back: Joe Cocker was starting a new world tour in Sheffield. The first of the city's two unrelated Cocker rock stars had been a regular around the city's pubs and clubs when I was at school, rejoicing in the gloriously sixties name of Vance Arnold. Even after he had hit the international big time by turning the jolly Ringo ditty of 'With a Little Help From My Friends' into a Deep South blues, he was reputed to put in impromptu appearances at a local music pub where Ron and I invariably failed to see him. Other reported sightings came, oddly enough, through my aunt who had worked with his Dad in the civil service and still kept in touch. 'Our John's bought us a colour television,' Mr Cocker senior had apparently told her, in the first flush of Joe's celebrity, 'I don't know about what else he's getting up to though.' The entire city seemed entranced at having produced a gas fitter who sounded like Ray Charles, even if not everyone was impressed by the wild hair and the even wilder arm movements on the air guitar. We didn't seem to have many stars in Sheffield. By the 1990s it all seemed a very long way off, an impression confirmed by the tenor of reporting in the non-Sheffield press at least. My Dad showed me the report on the forthcoming concert he knew I was going to when he spotted it in the 'Keighley News'. Looking up from his armchair with raised eyebrows and laughter bubbling from the corners of his mouth, his finger pointed out the headline. 'Wrinklies rock on,' it said, pitilessly.

Finding Sheffield Arena was not as simple as I expected. Stupidly, I thought I knew the entire area, imagining it as it was with the simple addition of a large auditorium. Once off the M1 in the early December darkness I was instantly lost in a sea of 'Toys R' Us' outlets and fast food joints lining the roads to the Arena where the steelworks had been. It seemed very, very strange. Inside the Arena things got odder still with more US-style fast food franchises and transatlantic accents booming out of the PA system over the bizarrely English-looking adverts for 'The Star' and 'The Green 'Un': it was as if a baseball stadium had suddenly whizzed in from Chicago or Baltimore, looking for an empty space to land. It was a relief when the lights went down and 'our Joe' appeared with his unmistakable Sheffield accent, despite the ranch in Colorado, and the voice that transported you straight back to the glory days of 'Steel City'. Looking round the audience, most of us by now middle-aged (certainly not 'wrinklies'!), it was impossible not to think how much had changed, how much Sheffield people would have been through which I had not had to share. Yet it seemed equally impossible that they too were not remembering, like me, when they had first heard these songs in the city where the steel guaranteed the future.

By the end of the concert, the force of the music and the power of the unchanged voice had produced a fierce emotional charge, transforming this arena which had all the intimacy of an aircraft hangar. In the inevitable finale of 'With a Little Help From My Friends' the audience stood as one, surging forward as far as the ranked seats would allow, whistling and clapping through the slow build of the introduction, roaring out in pure joy at the beautifully sung question in the first line of the song. It was as if we were all shouting, 'Give us an anthem, Joe!' - give us the time back, the hope, the certainties of twenty-five years ago. And just for a moment, as the music swelled upwards, it did indeed seem as if the concrete stadium had been transformed into a cathedral of memory, a place of better dreams. When the lights went up at last we looked around at one another, smiling sheepishly to discover our own tears in other peoples' eyes, the unmistakable look of shared pleasure in reliving and remembering. And then we filed out into the garishly-lit car parks, edging along bumper to bumper, across the gaping spaces where once all our history had been made.

46

'This time I'm going to have the best...'

Much to everyone's amazement, retirement turned out to be a total joy for my Dad. He had begun it, like so many, afraid of the unfilled time stretching before him and began to programme his days full of German and gardening classes. But, however interesting, they were not going to replace the role which had been lost when he stopped managing machine shops. It was not long, however, before he found an outlet for his skills. He joined Millhouses Park Bowling Club and discovered, unsurprisingly, a natural talent out on the crown greens beside the boating lake. In no time at all, his energies were happily employed as club secretary, organising teams, thinking up new competitions, collecting jokes and witticisms to use in his speeches on presentation evenings. Soon the sideboard had a bright collection of trophies replacing the refereeing cups which had long since been confined to a box in the spare bedroom. But, most of all, he found an immense pleasure in pottering around the garden, reading non-fiction and spending time with my Mum. They discovered a renewed companionship in talking together, enjoying on a far more regular basis the laughter they had always shared. 'Joyce is my best friend,' he would say, contentedly. Now that he had the time they could share so much more freely in his love of going out 'for a run' in his car.

All through the early years of his retirement, before the move to Keighley, he drove a bright blue Austin Allegro which he lovingly cared for and took on touring holidays of the West Country. Fourteen years old and still showroom-clean it became my first car not long after I finally passed my test. I went down to Sheffield for the 'test-drive' before he handed it over. I have no idea why he imagined that driving around in it together would let me see whether I liked it. It was exactly like being in Wales all over again. He never said a word as I crunched the gears ('oops, sorry!') and the car kangarooed its way around the estate. Just the hand clutching the front seat and the occasional sharp intake of breath were all that were required to convey his feelings. When we got home he wisely negotiated the car up the steep drive and under the carport and, on getting out, placed his hand solicitously on the bonnet. 'This car's still shaking, Susan,' he said, deadpan.

That was when he got his last car. It was a Nissan Micra, pale blue, neat brown seats. 'It's the top of the range,' he said, proudly. 'I thought, all my life I've always bought the cheapest. So I thought, right, this time I'm going to have the best.' He was already in his sixties with nine years of increasingly troublesome heart disease behind him: no doubt it had occurred to him that he wouldn't be repeating the purchase. He was proud of the car, of its nippiness and its reliability. He left the plastic on the seats for months after he bought it. I, meanwhile, would go into frantic sessions of cleaning out the car park tickets, the sweet wrappers and the drying banana skins from the passenger side of the Allegro every time I thought he might get anywhere near it.

The Micra just travelled around Yorkshire mostly, except for the epic journey they did with their old friends, Ron and Eunice Hubbard, to the Moselle region of Germany. Dad had always wanted to go back to Germany after the football trip, play with the language, enjoy the scenery. They spent ages enjoying the route-planning from the Hull-Rotterdam ferry, working out the packing. If you each take a plastic bin bag instead of a case, someone told my Dad, you can all get loads more things into a standard-size boot. He was delighted with this information and the subsequent fun of experimenting with it. He was equally pleased that Ron was a fellow driver and so would be good at helping with navigation and the tricky bits of driving on the right. He couldn't actually share the driving because he had never passed a test and always drove

Reliant Robins on his motor bike licence. Equally unhelpfully, it turned out, once in Holland, that he couldn't read a map either. Or, at least, that was my Dad's analysis of the situation. My Dad would describe reaching the peak of exasperation when, after some circuits of Rotterdam, they found themselves, on Ron's direction, driving along a canal towpath. It was left to me to imagine for my own pleasure poor Ron's exposure to the sharp-intake-of-breath scenario as they attempted to find Germany.

Midway through my Dad's retirement, with the move to Keighley, the car came into its own. It would come out every Friday 'for a run', allowing them to explore the many delights of an entirely new area. It would trundle over to Oakworth and away grounds all over the district for the bowls matches, as my Dad immediately reproduced his Millhouses form and in no time at all was running the Oakworth club. It would wait patiently in Morrison's car park whilst my Mum would pick up and reject ninety per cent of the produce on offer inside and Dad would faithfully push the trolley around in bemused frustration. After they decided to get more involved in their new community I would often drive back late from work and see the car parked outside Long Lee Chapel on the nights the men's fellowship held its meetings. It always felt reassuring to see the pale blue gleam and the F36 CHE under the street lamp. He was out doing things, everything must be okay.

47

'What do I have to do before you'll let me out of here...?'

Sometimes you wonder whether people pick their illnesses. Or at least, if a life-threatening condition is going to be unavoidable, there are undoubtedly some which seem more acceptable than others. Heart disease suited my Dad. Once he'd got over the initial shock that no-one can will their way into immortality he was rather good at it. At least, that was the way he saw it. He was, after all, a very fit man, a lifelong non-smoker and moderate drinker. If there were things he could do to help himself further, then he would. Long before it became universally fashionable, he started cutting out cheese and cream, cutting down on red meat.

Where he came a cropper was in the bits other people would take for granted, like seeing doctors or, especially, calling anyone out in the middle of the night. This produced a major divergence of opinion in my parents' house: if my Dad thought he was the model patient for never troubling the medical profession, my Mum had a rather different view. Whilst successive GPs remained quietly in their beds she was treated to almost twenty years of midnight anxiety at the severe angina which, in my Dad's view, was never quite bad enough. Through successive hours of the night, whilst he was busy toughing it out, she would be left to contemplate whether this would be the time she would always reproach herself for not taking matters into her own hands. But she never did. And they would both try to keep the worst of it from me, the distant daughter whose job seemed, increasingly, to be haranguing the pair of them down the phone.

The personality which produced the stoicism and the determined bravery in the face of pain, which made him the hero of the coronary care unit, was the same which made him utterly reckless and foolhardy when there were things he felt he ought to be able to do. The heart bypass operation provided a wonderful example of the Dr Jekyll side of him. He was determined to get through it as rapidly as possible, causing as little concern to anyone as he could manage. He was out of intensive care in half the expected time and, on his first meeting with the physiotherapist, asked, 'what do I have to do before you'll let me out of here?' 'You have to be able to climb up these stairs,' she said, pointing up two substantial flights. Off he went, inevitably, straight to the top, in an odd little foretaste of things to come. He was home by the end of the week, resolutely walking around, determined to get back in his car as fast as he could. It was a thoroughly triumphant business.

Yet the Mr Hyde aspect of all of this came out in his total impatience with himself whenever things took time. He had never been any good at waiting. Whenever he tried anything new he always had to be able to do it immediately or not at all. And this rarely caused him major problems because he was, after all, very gifted in his agility of mind and his extraordinary physical coordination. It was odd things like music which defeated him, abandoning the guitar, for example, when it proved impossible to learn it in twenty minutes. Or aspects of DIY when 'I'll have this done in half an hour' turned frustratingly into half a day. He never had time to take things steadily, most of all if the lack of speed was caused by any suggestion of weakness.

The combination of angina and DIY was a particularly lethal one which produced some of the oddest scenes in my relationship with my Dad. I once arrived in Sheffield on a Saturday lunchtime when he was in the middle of laying carpet tiles. He had set out the pattern across the middle of the through lounge but was left with all the tiles to cut around the edges. He looked visibly unwell as I walked through the door and saw him struggling on the floor with the steel rule and the Stanley knife. There seemed nothing for it but to acquire a rapid interest in carpet. 'Oh, I've always wanted to know how to do this, can I have a go?' I said, beginning an agonising afternoon of attempted straight cutting under his eagle-eyed supervision the length and breadth of the room.

It was carpet again, oddly enough, which later produced an identical scene in my own house. I had been stupid enough to say that the bedroom door wouldn't shut since the new carpet arrived and, in no time at all, he was standing at my front door with a saw in his hand. He unscrewed the bedroom door and lifted it down and it must have been then that the pains started. Sweat poured off him as he began to saw at the bottom of the door. But it would have been pointless trying to make him stop; it had to be another DIY lesson. 'Can I have a go? I've never been sure how to use a saw,' I said. 'I didn't think you could do it with your bad arm,' he replied, looking bothered. 'Can I try, if you watch me?' It seemed to go on forever, the attacking strokes of the saw at the ancient, solid wood, the shooting pains in the bad arm I wasn't going to admit to, the look of concern on his white, drawn face. As we stood the door back up I managed to look delighted at my achievement and thank him for showing me what to do. But it was not an experience I ever wanted to repeat; if he was dealing with illness by pretending it wasn't there it wasn't always so easy for the bystanders.

As time went on, after the bypass, through angiograms and angioplasty and constant medically-unsupervised attempts to reduce his medication, he never became any more accepting of the heart disease, except in aspects he could readily cope with. A rigorous attention to diet and exercise were elements which quite appealed to an ascetic streak in his make up; apart from this, he handled it by refusing to acknowledge its existence. He carried on, lugging heavy weights around when no-one was looking, surreptitiously painting ceilings when my mother was in town, and, amazingly, as time went on, having generally less trouble with the pains in his chest. And, in his 14th year of retirement, with the prescription of a new drug which its manufacturers promised would do away with the need for angioplasty, things got better still. Suddenly he was amazing us by managing an unprecedented six months with no angina at all. For the first time in a couple of decades I found myself looking ahead with some confidence.

48

'I understand you've a strong faith, Mr. Allott...'

It seemed such a good idea the minute I saw the brochure. The cruise around the Mediterranean looked delightful. It seemed the perfect answer for the golden wedding celebrations coming up the following year. We plunged into holiday planning. My Mum and Dad chose the itinerary they liked best and we looked at the pictures over and over again. It would be lovely to take them, to do something, for once in their lives, which would be 'no expense spared'. I just wanted to see the pleasure on their faces at the sights and the service and the excitement as the cruise ship sailed.

Long after we'd booked the holiday, all through that summer, the new 'miracle drug' Dad was taking for the heart disease was working its magic. There was no trace of the former illness, it was wonderful. It was also a bit eerie. After all this time, with all the damage to the heart that we knew about, it was as if he was suddenly cured. And then, one night, there was my Dad's voice on the phone. 'We want to come round for a minute. There's something we want to tell you.' We all sat round the kitchen table and my Dad, with his usual matter-of-factness, told us of the diagnosis of Parkinson's disease. I was devastated because I knew, immediately, that this illness, most certainly, was the wrong one.

It seemed to get worse very quickly. In no time at all the slight tremor I had noticed in his hand during the summer had turned into a periodic uncontrollable shake. His bold and flowing handwriting, always such a matter of pride, was becoming smaller and smaller with blots marring the cleanness of the page. There was a new hoarseness in his voice and a tightness in his throat, 'as if something's stuck in it,' he said. It was a symptom which disturbed him because he still loved to sing. After they moved up to Keighley my parents had joined the chapel choir. My mother would pick out the hymns they were rehearsing for Christmas or Easter on her small electric organ whilst my Dad, predictably, would just get annoyed if he couldn't pick up the tune in five minutes flat. In the spring before the cruise the men's fellowship was performing in a fundraising concert. He stood on the stage in the front row in his tie and his V-necked jumper, looking down at the music sheets, singing out as strongly as the Parkinson's would let him. 'I can hear you singing,' I said to him in the interval. 'Well, I don't know how you're managing that,' he said, but he beamed with pleasure all the same.

For this disease distressed him in a way the heart disease never did. He fretted that he couldn't cover up the symptoms, forever pressing his left hand over his right wrist or shoving the arm down the side of a chair where it wouldn't be seen. He hated what had happened to his writing. Scarcely a week went by without some intimation of a new deterioration. He clearly felt depressed at what he could already see. But he was already frankly terrified at what might be to come. He couldn't be brave in the face of this: for an impatient patient there could scarcely be anything worse than this steady descent into increasing incapacity. It offended against every fragment of his view of himself. So, as we came ever nearer to the cruise, I became convinced that we wouldn't be going. There were strange and baffling symptoms now. When anyone had ever asked my Dad how he was, he had always answered 'fine', even at times when he looked anything but. Now it was different. 'How are you?' we'd ask. 'Rubbish. I couldn't walk up the hill today,' he'd respond with uncharacteristic frankness. In the end even he had to admit defeat and call in the medics.

They admitted him for tests. He was pleased they were so thorough. 'You can't fault this for service,' he said, propped against his pillows as the plastic line fed him his blood transfusion. We fussed around with pyjamas and slippers, a better book to read.

Two days later he was feeling much better. When we walked into the ward he was just coming out of the day room, fully dressed. He had been watching the test match. His face lit up and he stepped over jauntily when he saw us. He had already phoned us after the doctors' rounds that morning to say that they had found 'signs of cancer'. But, by the evening, he clearly didn't want to talk about it any more. 'They said what they said because I asked the doctor what "suspicious" meant,' was all he volunteered. 'You're looking better, anyway,' we said, hopefully, scanning his bright, lively face. 'I feel better,' he said, 'I don't know what's going on on the inside though.'

And, after this, he was full of gaiety and a stream of the ironic little one-liners he was so good at. England, for once, were excelling themselves in the test match and he'd been glued to the set all day. 'Is it exciting?' I asked and he grinned, broadly, 'No, it's really boring. That's the whole point!' The little stories and the wisecracks went on, just as they had done for years, my Dad was bright-eyed, impish, taking a rise out of my Mum. She pretended to hit him for being cheeky, just like always. Until, as we left the ward, she murmured to me, 'Perhaps it's not right all this? He looks so well.'

At the end of four agonising days the verdict was delivered. We all sat in a little side room, out of the scurry of the ward, where dried flowers graced a lace-covered coffee table. Dad sat to one side, neat and small in his collar and tie. Mum sat beside him, shrunken against his arm, her hand clutching at him, still hoping for a reprieve. The medics were merciless. Within seconds of sitting down, the consultant, a man for whom the phrase 'dour Scot' must have been invented, was intoning words like 'inoperable tumour', 'secondaries in the liver', 'palliative care only'. 'I understand you've a strong faith, Mr. Allott, as I do,' he declared, and didn't quite add 'you're going to need it', but the words hung there in the air all the same.

There were questions and there were more 'plain-speaking' answers - and these words, 'plain speaking', were delivered, pitilessly, where the simple phrase, 'I'm very sorry' should have been. In his shock my Dad was suddenly calling this man 'sir', as if he were back with the bosses of the Light Machine Shop in the 1950s. Looking at my Dad, stunned but dignified, listening to his death sentence, all I could think was that he would have made two of this unbending professional man, for his insight, for his compassion, for his sensitivity. The wrong man was saying 'sir' here. As they got up to leave, the ward sister, the only one to bear an appropriate expression of sympathy, but silent, of course, in her necessary deference, offered us all tea. It arrived in a special china pot with matching cups and saucers which they obviously kept for moments such as these. 'We need the bad news teaset,' you could almost hear them saying. My parents sat together in the corner, huddled and close, slowly sipping away the end of fifty years together. Even with an entire history of illness, even when the evidence is staring you in the face, even then, there is no preparation for this moment.

After the verdict, the tests, the extra blood transfusion, we went to fetch him. A pale June sun glowed through the trees across the tarmac of the hospital car park. We walked out of the hospital slowly, saying little. Dad was looking around, perplexed that the world outside should seem the same. He reached out to take Mum's arm, automatically, to help her as they approached the steps, but he was the one who seemed unsteady, with his bright green pullover, so unlike him, not quite pulled down straight over his shoulders. He made an effort: 'Well,' he said, decidedly, 'I'm a complete failure!' and his habitual irony forced us to laugh. Back home he seemed suddenly weakened, knocked out at last by the body blow of the terminal diagnosis. He sat down heavily on the settee and, when Mum asked him if he felt all right, just whispered, 'I feel strange.'

Standing in the kitchen, making tea as an excuse to leave them together, I could hear him telling her that they would get out and do things, that he wasn't going to just sit there, that he wasn't just going to wait for it to happen. I was staring through the window at the garden he made from nothing, despite the angina, rushing to turn it into a 'joined-up garden', as he called it, so that it would be easy for Mum in case, one night, the heart gave out on him. And I was thinking that, in all these years of illness, it never ever occurred to me that one day I would be bringing him home to die.

And yet, even then, there was something about the way all this had happened which made it seem as if it was all for the best. In his refusal to see a doctor until the very last minute it was as if he had been determined to make sure there was no chance of a cure. If there was to be no way back from the stomach cancer, already so far advanced, it was doubtless no more than a man who was terrified of advancing Parkinson's had wanted. And besides, he was back on familiar territory, being courageous, being strong. Though there wasn't going to be a happy ending, at least it was his sort of disease. It was almost as if, like so many times before, he had got things to his liking.

49

'Capstick comes home...'

He was still talking about going on the cruise at first. 'I want to go. If I feel okay here I'll feel okay there. We should go.' We talked around and around it, deciding not to cancel immediately. 'We can look into the insurance. See how you feel, we don't have to tell anyone straight away,' I kept saying. But it was obvious that he was only delaying a decision so as not to disappoint us. Even at his brightest there were pains in his back and what he was calling 'discomfort' in his stomach, 'which I take it is to do with this problem I've got,' his only reference to the cancer. Most of all, he was so pitifully thin. I was astonished that I hadn't seen it before and yet, somehow, with his floppy jumpers and jackets, his persistent carrying of the heavy bags, he had pulled off a brilliant disguise. He was not going to be skipping up and down gangplanks in this condition.

The days passed slowly before the golden wedding. Sometimes it seemed improbable that he would get there at all. Christine, the liaison sister from Manorlands, the local hospice, would arrive for her regular Monday appointment, explaining about attendance allowance and the various options for nursing. He had assumed everyone ended up in hospital or a hospice but they were adamant that he could stay at home if that was what he wanted. On the other hand, the facilities at Manorlands sounded impressive. I walked into the house in the middle of this conversation to see my Dad turn round with a huge grin: 'it's so good, this place, forty per cent of people are completely cured!' We both burst out laughing and you could see the nurses, not used to him yet, were not at all sure it was a joke.

It didn't seem so bad somehow, on the days when he was taking charge like this, running the discussions the way he wanted them, keeping the laughter moving around the room or, most famously of all, supervising his own GP. Dr.England would carefully discuss the treatment with him and would then, more often than not, be treated to my Dad's view of his foolishness in continuing to play sport with a sports injury. On one occasion, as our good-natured doctor remarked that he was off to play squash, my Dad shot back, 'Well, if you're not going to follow my instructions, I don't want to see you again!' As far as I was concerned it wasn't the idea of his death that I was finding the most unbearable, it was watching him in the hours when he was defeated by exhaustion, struggling with a meagre plateful of food. And then, just as I would be trying to accustom myself to times like this, he would suddenly do something astonishing. Following me out to my car one afternoon he told me gleefully that he had bought my Mum a locket for the golden wedding: 'She went out on Monday and thought she'd left me at home and I dashed out in my car.'

Up at the Chapel they were planning a special afternoon to celebrate my parents' anniversary. My Dad was determined to be on top form, preparing a speech and an inevitable bit of comedy. He had decided to treat everyone to a rendition of 'Capstick Comes Home', Tony Capstick's wonderfully ironic parody of the sentimental northern Hovis adverts. He had done this once before at one of the men's meetings, getting everyone entirely seriously to practise the key bit of Dvorak's 'New World' symphony before launching into Capstick's monologue. Even then it had been a traumatic business providing him with the words. He had decided that, because of the Parkinson's, I would be much quicker than him at writing them down from the record. He sat on the floor beside the record player, taking the needle on and off the old forty-five. What had not occurred to either of us was that he would continually scrape the record because of the tremor in his hand. The middle of the piece was lost in an uncharacteristic fit of swearing and fuming, my Mum sitting tense in her chair, me scribbling away, deliberately ignoring him with a 'go on, what's the next bit?' It was just as well it was humorous. We finally made it to the last few lines with their mock nostalgia for all the 'olden days' had to offer: sickness, disease and Nazis.

He had looked up from the record player, his face wreathed in huge smiles at the words that were a rather closer reflection of his Sheffield reality than the brown bread and butter on the well-laid table.

I raced back early from the university to see the performance for the golden wedding party. There he was, standing behind the top table with its white cloths and the presentation flower basket, reading out the comic lines, clear and strong in his best Sheffield accent. My Mum looked happy and everyone clapped appreciatively; he was having a wonderful time. At the cutting of the cake, someone took a photograph which wound up in the local paper. They are smiling brightly, my Dad smart and sturdy in his jacket and tie. 'It's a golden day for Joyce and Frank,' the headline says. Only if you had known would you have noticed the slight strain around the eyes. Even for me, watching his delight at the afternoon's little kindnesses or the pleasure of holding his audience, it was, that day, unimaginable that in exactly two months from the golden wedding he would no longer be with us.

50

'This man is going to die with his collar and tie on...'

In the weeks that followed there were many performances to rival this one. If he could not avoid allowing my Mum and me to witness the miseries he endured as his condition worsened he was still determined to put on a show for the visitors. Even the medics were included in the list of people for whom he was determined to make an effort. Long after anyone else thought it necessary he would make sure he always looked his best before they arrived. As Christine told me later, 'I used to say back at the hospice, "this man is going to die with his collar and tie on!" ' Even if he could barely climb back upstairs when they had gone, even if the effort of speaking flattened him, he persisted in his neatness in his dress, his matter-of-factness about his death, his irony and jokiness on any available subject. On one classic occasion he was busy telling his GP that the persistent nausea he was suffering wasn't so bad; he could put up with it. 'Well, I don't want it!' the doctor exclaimed, and proceeded to pour over his pharmaceutical handbook, dropping in questions about 'waterworks and bowels', and producing the diverting information that astronauts are given drugs to stop bowel movements. 'Otherwise, they'd be gastronauts!' my Dad retorted, quick as a flash, and we all cracked up in a moment of pure joy at seeing him as himself again.

But behind the laughter, for me at any rate, was a frightening sense of responsibility as symptoms worsened, especially at the weekends when the trusted hospice team was unavailable. 'I just feel', I finally confessed to Dr.England, 'as if I am right at the edge of my competence here.' Though what I really felt, behind this restrained statement, was a kind of silent scream. Why, oh why, had

I wasted all those years getting languages degrees when I should so obviously have started out with nursing? How was it possible to know absolutely nothing about something so fundamental as dying? Why didn't we learn about this at school? Now that we no longer live in the cramped little houses by the steelworks, death, I had always been thankful to note, had ceased to be a commonplace. Yet, faced with the inevitability of it, I was appalled that knowledge my Grandma took for granted was a closed book to me. In this sudden wave of panic it felt as if home death, like home birth, was only for the reckless or intrepid. The doctor listened carefully and then said quietly, 'I think it will be this week, but I can't say for certain when someone has a spirit like that.' And, almost from the moment the words were spoken, my Dad began to give us a demonstration.

It was a Monday morning and there he sat on the settee, wrapped in his shiny blue dressing gown with his smart new slippers on his feet, treating us all to his finest performance. There was a steady stream of visitors: community nurses, friends, Christine paying her regular Monday visit as she had done since the diagnosis. Each one received tailor-made jokes and bits of bossing around: he was definitely going for the Academy Award. 'Sit down,' he said to me, as soon as I walked in, 'we were just talking about something interesting.' I sat on the floor. 'Have you heard this?' he asked, '"thou shalt not kill, but thou shalt not strive officiously to keep alive." It's the shortened, updated version of the Hippocratic oath. We've talked about this before, me and Christine. Because I've told her I don't want anybody keeping me hanging on unnecessarily.' We agreed that we both liked the word 'officiously'. 'It's good', we said, 'it's right.' I had always known that this would be how he would see things, that he would have no fear of saying so.

Christine told me later how unusual it was for anyone to be so up front. 'You just don't find yourself having that kind of conversation,' she said. But then, it was like everything else he was doing, such as repeating the favourite line he'd always had for her through these months, 'I'm fine in myself, apart from this cancer!' And his eyes glinted merrily as he grinned at her. He was so determined to be entertaining that we were all caught up in the show. Christine smiled. 'You're very stoical,' she said, and I added, 'Yes, we've had a lot of stoical over the years.' We all laughed at his rueful expression. He insisted on getting up, tottering across to the sewing basket on which he kept his diary. He wanted to write down when Christine would be coming next, just as he had carefully written every appointment since June. He wrote laboriously, hiding the book from her like a schoolboy and then showing it to her with a huge grin. She laughed uproariously when she saw it: he had put three kisses after her name. But the writing spidered across the line for Monday in a lack of precision so unlike him that we both knew there would not be a 'next week'. It was a grand final performance, though, and more than made up in panache for the lack of the collar and tie.

'So,' he summed everything up, 'I've sold my car, cancelled the insurance, told DVLC, cancelled my AA membership. Everything's done.' He smiled at me with satisfaction and leaned back against the cushions. Moments later, he slumped sideways and we urgently helped him to stretch out onto the sun lounger he had been using in recent days to watch TV. No-one expected him to see the hour out. And yet, unbelievably, twenty-four hours later he was still there, apparently unconscious. The nurses had been and gone, unhappy with the ad hoc arrangements, telling us they would get ambulance crew to get him up the stairs.

But, predictably, even now it is my Dad who has the last word. Suddenly wide awake, he is demanding to get back into his own bed, to have a wash, clean his teeth. Ernest, my Dad's brother, who has come rushing up here from Sheffield, looks across at me anxiously. And then my Dad, unbelievably, struggles to his feet. He stands, wavering, with Ernest's arms around him and begins to move around the sun lounger. 'I'm going upstairs,' he says. Ernest and I stand either side of him, holding the painfully thin arms, watching the feet on spindly ankles edge forward across the carpet. 'Have you ever done this before?' Ernest whispers to me, anxiously, behind his back. I shake my head, raising my eyebrows, but we are already at the door. In the hallway, my Dad, shaking from head to foot, stands looking up at the stairs. Suddenly, with an immense effort, he motions me aside, 'I want to hold that handrail,' he says. He reaches out, grasps it, the bones straining through the flesh of his hand, and suddenly sets off at a rush up the full flight, one, two, three, four, five and then two at a time as he nears the top and we scurry after him, dumbfounded. Standing at the top of the stairs as Ernest helps him into the bathroom, I am still reeling in amazement. I have never seen anyone climb stairs with their mind before.

When he gets into bed and lies back on the pillows his face is white, drained, expressionless. He closes his eyes. They will never open again. He will never move again of his own volition. But, as the last act in a world-class performance, this encore on the stairs will take some beating. I watch him, smiling at this gloriously characteristic ending. In this final, stolen morning he has shown us all the best of his life: the courage, the dignity and, above all, the indomitable will. It would be hard to find a better moment than this final triumph at which to let the curtain fall.

51

'More tons of steel are produced in Sheffield today...'

It was more than a year later, on the eve of a new century, before I came back to Sheffield and I was surprised at what I found. The devastation of the collapse of steel had given way to a different, brighter world, immediately visible from the train as it slowed towards Midland Station. Gradually, over all these years, the east-end spaces where the steelworks once rose had been filled in with system-built warehouses and showrooms, their eye-catching signs calling out brightly to the passing traffic. And if the 45,000 who used to work in steel a mere thirty years ago had been reduced to less than 8,000, maybe it didn't matter so much any more: at a casual glance, the city at the end of the 20th century was looking much like any other in this country which had so thoroughly 'restructured' its industrial past. The era of boarded shop-fronts and perpetual 'closing down' sales had given way to a re-emerging civic confidence as clear and powerful as the water cascading through the bold new square where once the roses of the Peace Gardens bloomed. The city centre shops were as glossy and predictable as in any other High Street: the same gaggles of smart and purposeful young women striding through the dripping December streets, the same white-faced young men with dogs on bits of rope huddling in doorways behind the change in a styrofoam cup.

But it felt good to be home. I couldn't wait for my city centre stop as the supertram glided impressively down West Street past the old Employment Exchange where my Granddad in his flat cap and muffler had queued so fruitlessly several light years ago. I jumped off at the next to walk through the back streets in the pouring rain and enter the city from the far side of the City Hall.

There was the door where Ron and I had queued to watch folk concerts in the Memorial Hall. There was the entrance we had all piled through for school speech days, and the smell of the sodden stonework brought back the memories of being made to learn the school hymn off by heart, watching numbly as the head of school governors in her extravagant picture hat made a meal of presenting the prizes. Up above the Moor, the city's coat of arms hung proudly in the centre of strings of Christmas lights, as determined in their local patriotism as ever. And even if the landmarks had gone - no more Goodwin Fountain at the top of Fargate, no more 'hole in the road' – it didn't take long to realise that all the corporate identities and mission statements of nineties Britain had not managed to stop the traditional local endearment, 'duck', still being good customer relations in this city's shops.

It was whilst I was looking at the shelves of local publications in the station bookstore as I waited for my train back to Keighley that I came across it again. For the third time in as many months someone had said to me, or I had found myself reading, this same statement: 'Surprising as it may seem, more tons of steel are produced in Sheffield today than at any time during the history of the steel-making industry in the city.' Staring out of the railway carriage as we picked up speed, imagining the long-gone machine shops along the Don Valley, I felt unease at the pride in the statement. Demolition, mass unemployment, increased efficiency, higher tonnage: I wanted to believe in the message of good news but struggled to take the words at face value. Had automation really won the day after all? If he had still been with us, my Dad would have known why it felt as if there was something wrong with the picture. Perhaps, if I could only concentrate on this now-transformed valley where he spent his working life, I could still conjure up his response.

Across the darkness of the winter landscape, where the brake lights gleamed like Christmas baubles on the wet roads out to the motorway at Tinsley, through the double glass of the train window,

I was imagining holding the book out to him, listening intently for his response.

'What do you reckon to that then? Do you think that's right?'

And, suddenly, it is as if he is looking up from the page, taking off his reading glasses:

'It may well be right, I wouldn't dispute it,' and he smiles his wry, knowing smile, 'but it wasn't the tonnage we were famous for.'

52

'Every day's a bonus...'

If I missed his knowledge and his observations, I missed far more my Dad's philosophy as time went by. Knowing that he had been blessed with many more years of life than he had had a right to expect, he became unafraid of death. In his survival of the heart disease, in his intense enjoyment of each day, he had become a contented man. 'Every day's a bonus,' he would regularly announce, decidedly. Throughout his life he had expected little and his pleasures had always remained modest. A nice garden, a small family car, holidays in chalets and caravans, days out locally and simple meals in ordinary cafes, these were the mainstays of his life. What was extraordinary about him all came from inside, through his kindness, his wit, his impish playfulness and his wisdom.

Perhaps much of the wisdom was the wisdom of age and illness, of understanding at last that there are limitations. As he would say to me, watching my heady professional progress, 'be careful, don't do what I did, don't go thinking you're indispensable'. If he had driven himself into a catastrophic heart attack he had had the leisure to reflect on the folly of such worldly pursuits. By the time I was heading down a road of similarly potential disaster he was already waiting, cup of tea and special cake in hand, to dispense his insights into the pitfalls of success. He had learned that there were more enduring things in life than reaching out for the other end of the rainbow.

What would he have made of this 21st century Sheffield he never got to see, the city which, in the end, drew me back home? He would, I'm sure, have been pleased to see the smart new buildings, would have loved the gorgeous Winter Gardens and the Millenium

Galleries. He would have been amazed and no doubt tickled to see people sipping wine at pavement cafes in the continental style, glad to see the new events and festivals, new businesses opening up. But he would have been stunned by the need for food banks, horrified by the crisis of homelessness. He would have been appalled at the depth of the misery created by policies of austerity; he never believed in politicians' protestations that social improvements could not be afforded. 'They can always find money for bombs,' he would say.

Yet I think he would have acknowledged that the shock and depression of the years which followed the collapse of steel had, by and large, given way to a new spirit. The stuffing might have been knocked out of us but, in the end, the sense of hope did begin to come back. Most of all, he would have been thrilled to see the 'Women of Steel' statue and the recognition which my Mum finally received for her work in the war. Though I had to smile as I received the medal on her behalf after she too was no longer with us. I could hear exactly what my Dad would have said: 'So I worked at Firth Brown's for forty-four years and you were there for five, Joyce, and they've given you a medal? That doesn't sound quite right to me!' But there would have been no mistaking the pride and the love in his voice for his 'best friend'.

What no-one tells you about losing someone close is how the little things affect you most of all, how the apparently trivial details of a life suddenly become the memories which make you catch your breath. I always seemed to be looking for him in those first years after his death, scanning the faces of elderly men in crowds. But none of them had that jaunty air, that sudden huge smile when he spotted you, those bow legs we used to look for running the line on 'Match of the Day'. And none of them, in the end, could ever be as thin as my father became, walking on bravely in his flapping holiday trousers. But I couldn't help stare at these grey-haired figures, stooping to catch what their wives were saying as they walked through the middle of town. I couldn't help but notice the affecting details of age I never saw before: the trilbies and the glasses, the cardigans and the gnarled fingers, above all, the shocking frailty of yesterday's 'big men'. And, as I watched them, in couple after couple with their shopping bags and parcels, I found myself wondering how much longer their neatly-permed wives would have them to nag at and fuss over, how soon the years of missing the companionship would start.

I looked for him in fragments of his writing, notes and jottings that fluttered unexpectedly from between the covers of his well-loved books. Most of all, I looked for him in collections of old songs, listening out for the lines where I could still hear his voice soaring up high as he walked between the kitchen and the living room: 'deep in my heart, dear…'. Down would go the ivory-handled knives and forks onto the checked tablecloth and out he would wander, 'de - eep in my heart, de - ear...'. In the cafe where Nat King Cole was singing his favourite, 'Unforgettable', or looking out at the sea over the Spa where the Scarborough Spa Orchestra was playing selections from Rodgers and Hammerstein, I could still hear his sweet, high tenor. But, in the end it turned out, to my surprise, that I was looking in all the wrong places.

53

'Forest, bears...'

In a provincial backwater in the heart of Russia a small town huddles above a river cliff. In early spring, pallid sunlight slants through the birches on the cowslips and ajuga scattered yellow and blue across the steep, grassy banks. When I first saw this place livestock wandered at will across the rutted tracks which passed for roads whilst, in the centre of town, the occasional car swerved around giant potholes which seemed to defy all attempts at progress. In 1906, the local newspaper recorded, an Englishman emerged from the cafe of the town's one hotel, stumbled into one of these potholes after heavy rain and drowned; the first mention of my homeland in the annals of this place. This is Chekhov country where the white cherries blossom still and where, when the sky turns threatening, it is impossible to tell which are snowflakes and which petals as they blow into your hair. And, in one of many anonymous grey blocks of flats, on the brow of the hill above the old wooden houses, sits a man who, whatever he is feeling, is stoical and dignified, who calls pain 'discomfort', who knows how to give a bravura performance, telling his funny stories, cutting pieces of special cake.

'Sue, tell me why you first came here,' he says, 'why was it Russia?' So I begin at the beginning, as in all the best tales. 'Well, it all started when I was six and my Dad brought a globe home one night...' And when I get to the bit about 'forest, bears', he makes me start all over again, because he thinks it is such a wonderful story, so unexpected. For, of course, from his side of the Iron Curtain, he has been brought up to see us as the Cold War enemy too. So I explain about the Germans at Caister Camp, how my Dad had made friends with lads just like himself, how it had changed his view of the world forever: 'people are the same the world over, it's not people that want war.' It was never about politics for my Dad; it was always about peace. Much later Mikhail tells me what the story immediately made him think: 'your Dad's still with you and he knows what you're doing, that's for certain. It's as if he's here, or has been here – look at his really positive attitude towards Russia, the way he brought you the globe and what he told you.' And if, at the time, I just smile, later I can't help but wonder if there is something in what he is saying.

It is late in the afternoon of a golden summer's day when we walk into the garden of the house where I will stay, a place to translate and write, where we will sit out under the apple trees as the meteor showers streak across the July sky. The house is tiny and dark and, like so many old houses in rural Russia, there is no running water and nothing but an earth closet at the end of the garden path. But it will be fine, I will manage, and there is a table under the trees where I can work. It all feels very straightforward and matter-of-fact until I walk down the garden and open the door of the tiny wooden dacha. Behind the lace at the windows there is room only for a chair and a bed, crammed in under the huge pine beams of the ceiling. But on the far wall, above the bed, I can scarcely believe what I am seeing. There is a carpet tacked to the wall in the Russian manner. And woven into the carpet is a picture: forest, bears.

Long after midnight I am standing on the dacha steps as the moon comes rising over the pines. In its gleam, the shapes of the bears on the wall stand out for a moment before the clouds pass over. And I am smiling, reflecting how much my Dad would enjoy what I am thinking now: that this is the place he set me searching for from a Sheffield council house so many years ago, that it was his tolerance and openness that made this improbable path seem so natural to me. And a song is instantly there, as always. It is Richard Tauber's song from the old musical, 'White Horse Inn', but the voice is my Dad's singing 'Serenade', the song about the moonlight. 'It's nice music, this, isn't it, Sue?' I can hear him saying, as he always said, and the smile grows wider and wider as the melody plays on.

* 9 7 8 1 9 1 3 4 2 5 0 8 1 *

BV - #0050 - 230222 - C8 - 229/152/13 - PB - 9781913425081 - Gloss Lamination